Virtual Engagement

Virtual Engagement

Managing Seamless Marketing with Technology

Rajagopal

Distinguished Professor of Marketing
EGADE Business School
Tecnologico de Monterrey
Santa Fe Campus, Mexico City
Mexico
&
Visiting Professor
Department of Administrative Sciences
Boston University, Boston, MA

BEP
BUSINESS EXPERT PRESS
Leader in applied, concise business books

Virtual Engagement:
Managing Seamless Marketing with Technology

Cover design by Cassandra Kronstedt

Interior design by S4Carlisle Publishing Services, Chennai, India

First published in 2025 by
Business Expert Press, LLC
222 East 46th Street, New York, NY 10017
www.businessexpertpress.com

ISBN-13: 978-1-63742-858-0 (paperback)
ISBN-13: 978-1-63742-859-7 (e-book)

Business Expert Press Marketing Collection

First edition: 2025

10 9 8 7 6 5 4 3 2 1

EU SAFETY REPRESENTATIVE
Mare Nostrum Group B.V.
Mauritskade 21D
1091 GC Amsterdam
The Netherlands
gpsr@mare-nostrum.co.uk

To Arati

Contents

List of Figures and Tables

Figures

Table

Preface

Continuous evolution of information and communication technologies (ICT) has significantly penetrated digitalization of conventional business processes and the Internet of Things (IoT) concept in business. The competitive engagement of firms with virtual technologies tends to unveil new business models (BMs) within hybrid environments. This phenomenon has extensively contributed to the continuous growth of the new business economy in a hybrid environment. Such business impetus is developed around so-called metaverses. In the cyber–physical ecosystem, BMs have been developed as a combination of physical- and virtual-world mechanisms that help in developing social and economic values. The economic creation and value capture at the crossroads of physical and virtual economies today are contributed through the cyber revolution comprising artificial intelligence (AI), augmented reality (AR), virtual reality (VR), and metaverse (Mancuso et al. 2023). BMs based on digital technologies and within hybrid environments are increasingly spreading to facilitate innovative products and services offerings, collaborations, and transactions through new interaction modalities within community-based and crowd-based contexts. Therefore, virtual BMs are challenging and innovating the traditional market dynamics, which not only augments profit but also helps in managing unforeseen business conditions. Consequently, firms implementing virtual BMs have been successful in reducing the cost, time, and risk factors in business and enhancing market-oriented innovations in the digital and virtual environments (Jingyao et al. 2022).

Core Arguments

AI and machine language (ML) technologies have revolutionized managerial decision-making through interactive platforms, which are transforming the decision-making processes by inducing advanced learning capabilities. The convergence of AI and ML are highly personalized, based on manager's interest in resolving organizational conflicts and making decisions through AI platforms (Stokel-Walker and Van Noorden 2023). A pre-trained model of AI and ML helps in developing a logical framework with a large amount of verbal and nonverbal data to enable decision-making in a highly sophisticated manner. The advanced capabilities of AI and ML allow managerial decisions to administer situation-based decisions by matching problems, needs, and solutions. However, the impact of Generative AI as an outgrowth of AI and ML has limited implications in complex business situations, as AI offers a large number of options that can be categorized as choice overload in managerial decisions (Scheibehenne et al. 2010). Managerial decision-making conventionally depends on organizational knowledge, intelligence, and culture, which affects the cognition process at both the managerial and organizational levels. Previous studies have shown that superimposing technology on managerial decision-making often does not match with the intellectual bandwidth of managers and stakeholders in deriving the sense of commonality (Jussupow et al. 2021). Therefore, synchronizing meta-cognition and meta-learning is a major challenge in technology-based decision-making and making decisions compatible with tangible and quantifiable improvements (Sturm et al. 2023).

There are many embedded technical and organizational aspects that affect managerial decision-making by utilizing the AI and ML platforms. The managerial trust is largely affected by the choice spread and overload in decision-making while resolving the organizational problems at various levels. Though AI and ML offer great potential to craft managerial decisions by augmenting the verbal and nonverbal data, influence managers in business decision-making require total quality assessment and transparency at various levels of decisions (Coombs et al. 2020). AI embeds several unspoken conflicts, which often restricts decision-makers from trusting data and gaining confidence in the advice given by the AI to reach the effective decision-making in real-world organizational contexts (Fügener et al. 2021). Advancement in ICT has been vital in knowledge management practices, which enable architecting the managerial decisions through knowledge distillation from the metaknowledge repositories (Zhu et al. 2023). Knowledge distillation is supported by technology platforms to resolve complex problems and helps managers to take flexible decisions through organizational knowledge networks. Crowdsourcing and collective intelligence also help in building metaknowledge reposi-tories by blending corporate and stakeholder information (Wang et al. 2014). AI supplements managerial knowledge and impacts problem-solving scenarios through quality function deployment. Consequently, the complexity in decision-making is resolved through AI platforms in-tegrating trade-offs between accuracy and complexity in decision-making by improving managerial behavior through knowledge transformation.

In managing the virtual businesses marketing, managers strive to build branded experiences among consumers in a virtual space through social media channels, which challenge stakeholders to engage in novel ways to enhance attitudes and encourage positive behaviors toward the virtual brands. The virtual BMs offer immersive and interactive encounters with the consumers and business partners, including supply chain players. VR technology is a promising tool for managers to create these experiences, as evidenced by the increasing and successful VR marketing applications used by the e-commerce firms. Though there are many studies published on the role of ICT and technology-led marketing applications, little guid-ance is available on how the advanced technological experiences in market-ing can be strategically designed to create favorable customer perceptions, attitudes, and behaviors. Aligned with a human-centered technology and experience-based marketing approach, the virtual business is regarded as a real-time, immersive, and interactive multisensory experience situated in an artificially induced and responsive three-dimensional computer-generated virtual environment (de Regt et al. 2021). As consumers increasingly interact on digital platforms with brands; relationships are es-tablished, enhanced, and strategically nurtured through the customer re-lationship management (CRM) technology, including experience-sharing on social media channels. Crowd behavior and the quality of collective intelligence also help in strengthening the virtual business perspectives among stakeholders. Such customer touchpoints have given rise to the virtual economy, where customers increasingly go beyond mere consump-tion, experiencing novel ways of buying transactions. E-commerce tech-nology provides a promising avenue to the firms to create fully immersive, multisensory customer experiences (Kang et al. 2020).

Changing cyber–physical attributes of the marketplace with increas-ing use of ICT and virtual application are rapidly transforming their business into an online platform in developing countries. Such change is evident in the community-centric products like health, food, textiles, and so on in the emerging markets. Such transformation is also driven by the societal changes that reflect in the social and sectoral service system (Jokinen et al. 2019). This has induced companies to do more careful and long-term strategic planning on their neighborhood business orientation and service provision to assure an acceptable profit level, empower customers, and cocreate values. However, consumers in low-income geo-demographic segments require access to the Internet and proximity to delivery points. Virtual business firms, which operate on economies of scale, use hubs-and-spoke supply chain model to connect niches and effectively serve customers through local partners. At the same time, a flexible matrix of stakeholder engagement, business leaders, and managers around the world share a common understanding of corporate strategy. Some customer-centric companies practicing virtual marketing approach maintained consistent practices toward engaging high-quality managers and linking decentralized neighborhood groups through the profit-with-purpose goals of marketing (Maljers 1992). Advancement of ICT has driven the need for a coherent outreach strategy, fresh skills, and adaptive tactics through digitalization and networking approaches in business. Drawing on the e-commerce benefits, the changes brought by digital networks and social media platforms have revealed the ways by which managers can take advantage of proximity BMs. As most emerging Business-to-Consumer (B-to-C) and Business-to-Business (B-to-B) firms are transforming their conventional BMs to virtual platforms, their approach to customer outreach is linked with the social media to identify new opportunities and drive customer engagement. The most successful firms focus on community management as a dedicated function by combining marketing, public relations, and information technology skills (Kane et al. 2009).

Firms began to adopt "persuasive technologies" in business in the early 21st century as an outgrowth in computer science and presented them as intentional devices or applications to change human attitudes and behaviors. E-commerce websites, social media, video games, and VR applications have been designed to transform behavioral change among consumers. The transcending immersive relationship of consumers with the brand significantly impacts customer attitudes toward the brand

(Jolink and Niesten 2021). With the increasing applications of AI, AR, and VR technologies, consumer experiences had been immersive in nature. However, sustainability, business, and sustainable behavior in business are relatively late adopters of VR technology. VR found momentum on tourism in the 1990s illustrating how the 3D visualizations of tourist destinations could potentially reduce the carbon footprint of vulnerable environments. The 3D visualizations were in fact 2D environments on-screen, allowing visitors to experience on-screen what they could expect in reality (Wei et al. 2019).

As VR and sustainability in business have entered the new millennium, the simplified representations of reality in VR gradually created nonexisting "ecotopias." The illusion of "being there" was initially generated through multisensory input, such as seeing, feeling, and hearing digitally simulated information, and, later, "presence" was associated with personal decision-making in, and interaction with, the virtual environment (Weech et al. 2019). The ability to influence consumer emotions related to brands through VR has affected individual attitudes and generated awareness about changing the collective behavior toward e-commerce and virtual business platforms (Fauville et al. 2020). Virtual business integrating virtual shopping today is a latitudinal approach, which enhances the outreach of customers through effective consumer advocacy, diffusion of collective intelligence, and influencing consumers through the crowd behavior. Due to the increasing dependency on social media marketing and network marketing trend, the latitudinal proximity in business markets is rapidly reducing. Such shifts in consumer marketing have significantly affected the buying behavior of consumers (Tiwary et al. 2021). Destination region image is neither a simple aggregation of the images of member cities nor dictated by the image of a single well-known destination. Both the physical and conceptual connections among multiple shopping destinations exhibit the collective behavior of shopping and consumer connectivity. Social networks have been primarily viewed as platforms to explore the changing consumer behavior and align new business opportunities or partners by rebuilding relationships through continuous communication. Proximity marketing is thus evolving as a popular networking longitudinal and latitudinal marketing approach that enables a better construction of the consumers' belief systems (Muller and Peres 2019).

Virtual business propagates through virtual communities, which include tools ranging from discussion boards to massive multiplayer online roleplaying games and virtual realities. The business world believes today that virtual communities can leverage consumers and consumer data. However, the benefits of such communities have not always been experienced by many online B-to-C firms. The theories of social contracts and trust can be reviewed in a contemporary context to endorse how firms can successfully participate in virtual communities. These theories need to be critically examined from the perspective of peer orientation, consumer interest, relationship-effects, and IoT-driven social groups, which encourage consumer participation in virtual business. The virtual value chain platforms provide an instructive background to understand which firm activities are candidates for being included in virtual communities. Success in virtual communities depends on stakeholder contribution, dedication of resources, building a critical mass, and matching community and business needs (Spaulding 2010). Most successful e-commerce companies like Amazon and Alibaba develop their marketing and operations strategies by understanding the behavioral proximities of consumers. The concept of proximity marketing is contextual to the consumer-centric marketing, brand socialization, and socio-ethical values. Proximity marketing includes social media marketing practices by invoking the concept of value or virtue that considers freedom of speech of consumers, crowd behavior, collective intelligence, and transparency in communication (Alan Stainer 1998).

Market competition is a dynamic process stimulated by continuous growth in innovation and technology. The changing market competition affects the consumption pattern and behavior of various segments of customers. Consequently, market trends and consumer behavior are continuously changing, and social media is playing a critical role in determining marketing decisions. Proximity marketing helps the companies acquire customers and gain competitive advantage. However, volatility of customer markets can have significant negative effects on risk-averse market share, profitability, and brand equity of companies. However, volatility is one of the most important concepts in competitive growth theory. The central argument of this theory is that the companies operating in a competitive business environment consider customer preferences, innovation, technology, and growth-related investments. Emerging markets are facing value-based competition as the value-for-money customer segment is expanding latitudinally (Rajagopal 2021). In this business dynamics, success is not guaranteed to the companies irrespective of their size, resources, and power. Reviewing several attributes of business today, questions often arise like why businesses fail and whether design matters. SMART (strategic, measurable, accessible, responsive, and trustworthy) and socially connected business designs raise a broad set of new strategic choices converging the attributes of markets, social responsiveness, and customer values to help companies perform as a corporate citizen (Rajagopal 2021). Creating social and customer values and securing competitive advantage by acquiring new capabilities to reshape industries present increasing challenges for companies in emerging markets.

Virtual marketing has always been at the edge of ambiguity of the stakeholders as it trolled between two constructs of *tangibility* and *intangibility*. *Tangible* constructs are actual, such as physical objects with touch, feel, and pick sensitivity, while the *intangible* stimulants in marketing can be experiences such as using virtual assistants like Siri or Alexa, which are unreal but deemed real nonetheless because stakeholders and customers can interact with them to gain information. In addition, *Possible* constructs may have a pseudo effect of real business and exhibit a real-like market situation. For example, metaverse can be the possible *virtual* business construct that attracts both internal (employees) and external (investors) stakeholders beside customers. The concept of reality is an enduring domain, which induces design thinking and cyber–physical boundaries. In virtual business, reality refers to the actual, physical world that exists and that people navigate every day. This reality has given rise to all virtual business activities despite the growing concerns on possible constructs as an outgrowth of the advancement of ICT. The majority of commercial transactions in retail, manufacturing, and services, therefore, have a hybrid business with the physical copresence of people and objects (Farshid et al. 2018).

In customer-centric companies, business design perspectives are becoming central to the stakeholders, networks, and communications. Several business designs have emerged over time as a collective communication approach in business organizations involving decision-makers, employees, customers, and stakeholders. The involvement of people in business has been practiced in many companies as a crowd participation approach in design thinking, developing print and digital commercials for products and services, and in value cocreation programs. Engaging consumers in relationship management and business operations has benefited consumers in updating their real-time knowledge on market and consumption needs (Kietzmann 2017). Therefore, companies should develop task–media fit models of communications by adopting an interactive approach to influence customer relationships and consumption behavior. Task–media fit model manifests in articulating communication and relationship marketing strategies through interactive tools such as mobile messages, e-mails, personalized meetings, seminars, and disseminating information through reports and graphic illustrations. Task–media fit theory explains the convergence of communication tasks such as sharing experience, sales data, future product or services marketing plans, or technical data, associated with products and users with the appropriate media (e.g., e-mail, text, interactive online sessions, or face-to-face meetings). These approaches drive proximity in marketing as an effective strategy to develop confidence, conformity, and cooperation among consumers (Mason and Leek 2012).

Most organizations have realized today that staying in business as learning organizations helps them to grow competitively and consistently in the marketplace. Design thinking in business has been conceived as an essential tool for simplifying the business operation by interlinking organization, society, and stakeholders and by more comprehensively humanizing the business. The extended principles of design thinking in businesses converge with the market attributes (market players, ethics, and business growth), social responsiveness (marketing with purpose), and value propositions of customers. The philosophy of inclusive business advocates the people-led win-win business model to lead the market (Desai 2014). The concept of virtual proximity in businesses rose to prominence by the end of the 20th century, as crowd workspaces and sharing of experience offered deep and meaningful relationships between customers and employees of the company to increase the collective psychodynamics. The activities performed by the firms in developing new customer relationships are often built around efficient communication tasks to drive interpersonal communications, confidence, and cognitive bonding. Brand marketing is characterized by extensive interpersonal communications not only between buyers and sellers but also between wide-ranging functions performed by the actors at back- and front-stages (Rajagopal 2011).

Conversational interaction is an important tool to develop proximity and can be achieved by understanding how companies can forge authentic and durable brand relationships with the various segments of consumers when they aggregate cyber–physical marketing. Such interactions allow firms to not only understand the customer insights but also realize the power of cocreation and coevolution of business in the competitive marketplace (Livingston and Opie 2019). A hybrid conversational-communication style drives positive customer–brand relationships and helps firms to evaluate the geodemographic association of brands with the consumers. Firms can develop proximity index based on communication, interactivity, cognitive variables, relationship drivers, competitive touchpoints, and business growth. In addition, cocreating customer service and relationship hubs fosters marketing, public relations, and communications strategies to develop a positive consumer–business helix and ecosystem (Schultz et al. 2011). This book argues that until companies understand the contribution of technology-led marketing and inculcate stakeholder value, the true growth in business is unlikely under the rapidly changing technology.

Continuous learning and effective knowledge management foster a synergetic symbiosis between information technology and managerial and organizational cognition. The advancement in information technology has significantly contributed to managerial decision-making and knowledge management in organizations (Carayannis 1999). AI has emerged as a new facet of information technology and has overpowered the conventional practices of managerial and organizational cognition (Helfat and Martin 2015). The Generative AI is a recent outgrowth of crowd-based AI, which is commonly used in the managerial decision-making process. Consequently, both AI and knowledge management can be perceived as strategic enablers of managerial and organizational cognition that contribute to collaborative learning and developing repositories of metaknowledge diffused through management networks in new-generation organizations. Generative AI is an innovative phase of AI that serves as a next-generation intelligent agent in developing knowledge management repositories in an organization to support managerial decisions (Melumad et al. 2020).

The Concept Map

The principal discussion standpoints of this book include the following: (a) attributes of virtual business firms and adaptation to cyber–physical marketing technology and (b) the disruptive spin of marketing strategies around the 3C factors—Cyber–business competition, Convergence of innovation and technology, and Consumer ecosystems as illustrated in Figure 1. In the rapidly changing market environment, firms face increasing challenges in focusing on a virtual business model. Consequently, firms use the strategy–track approach by integrating the customer track (preferences and trends), competitive edges (competitiveness, shopping drives, and new attractions), and leading cyber–physical space in managing the virtual business. Most B-to-C and B-to-B firms are engaged in spinning the strategy–track approach to gain market competitiveness (Lord et al. 2002). The discussions in this book are connected to four principal domains: virtual competition, strategy versus tactics, virtual market ecosystem, and technology management contextual to the core theme of this book, namely, virtual business. The book is divided into five chapters intertwining the concepts and cases across these discussion domains as exhibited in the Figure P.1.

The discussion on virtual marketing in this book begins by analyzing the ICT and major AI-driven trends in the 21st century. Discussion on the fast-track marketing trend based on e-commerce using technology tools is central to Chapter 1, which focuses on synchronizing virtual business design using advanced ICT tools, collective intelligence, and convenience marketing by developing an appropriate technology–business fit (Gilboa et al. 2019). The fast-track development in e-commerce is witnessed in the market, as emerging B-to-C and B-to-B firms are swiftly moving to virtual space using the AR and VR devises to push breakthroughs in retailing. This chapter discusses the role of AI, AR, and VR on e-commerce performance, technology-led business modeling, and

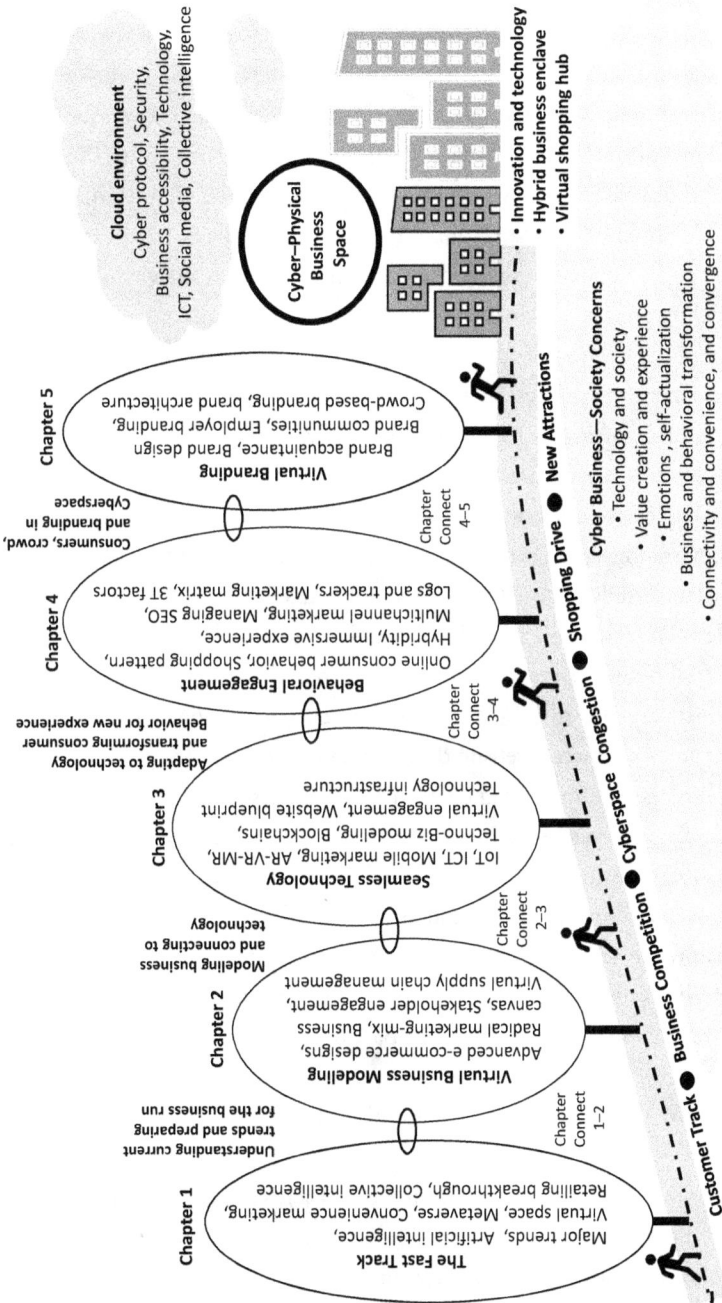

Figure P.1 Discussion paradigm of the book

managing convenience marketing using innovative technology platforms like metaverse. As the rapidly evolving technology is symbiotic to the cyber–physical marketing trends, Chapter 2 focuses on the strategic (long-term) virtual business modeling using advanced e-commerce designs and radical marketing-mix comprising 27 elements overshadowing the conventional 4Ps—Product, Price, Place, and Promotions. This chapter also discusses the business canvas–marketing modeling fit to improve the performance of virtual marketing. Emerging trends on virtual supply chain (VSC) management and their integration with the virtual business modeling are also discussed in Chapter 2. The e-commerce's major challenge of connecting people to business woven around the cyber–physical engagement of consumers, as well as the behavioral proximity emphasizing the role of interactive marketing in cyberspace with the support of ICT, constitute the core discussion in Chapter 2.

Chapter 3 discusses the seamless ambience of virtual business technology that has grown in the 21st century, which spread across IoT, and the Metaverse Reality (MR) beyond AR and VR. The contemporary tools to develop techno-biz models in specific sectors such as consumer health and well-being, electronic home appliances, fashion, value, and lifestyle products are also discussed in this chapter. In addition, Chapter 3 provides an e-commerce website development blueprint that guides the new entrepreneurs in managing e-commerce business. In addition, Chapter 3 discusses concepts related to virtual block chains, technology infrastructure, and consumer–firm virtual engagement. Discussions on innovating virtual marketing practices and push-pull effects support the conversations on the techno-biz modeling presented in this chapter. Arguments and critical discussions in this chapter also include the long-term (strategic) versus short-term (tactical) impact of virtual marketing on the competitiveness and performance of customer-centric businesses (Juntunen et al. 2019). Discussions on developing the technology-led e-commerce strategy to gain competitiveness and convergence of virtual marketing approaches with customer value are spread across all chapters in the book. Accordingly, the customer-centric discussion domain of virtual market system with focus on consumer outreach, business expansion, and innovation and technology is presented in Chapter 4, the central focus of which is behavioral engagement. Chapter 4 discusses online consumer behavior, virtual shopping patterns, and immersive experience in virtual marketplace. The hybrid BMs integrating cyber–physical infrastructure meet the increasing challenges of changing market ecosystem. The cyber–physical triadic marketing-design strategy comprising design-to-market, design-to-society, and design-to-value as an innovative approach for the firms is also discussed in Chapter 4. Besides the customer-centric techno-economic and socio-psychological perspectives of virtual marketing scenarios, managing search engine optimization techniques and analyzing the transaction logs and supply chain trackers from the manufacturing point to the point of delivery are categorically addressed in this chapter. In addition, the chapter discusses concepts like marketing value matrix, multichannel marketing and the 3T elements comprising Time, Trust, and Transparency that significantly affect the virtual marketing process. The last discussion domain on virtual branding is central to the conversation and arguments in Chapter 5, which portrays virtual brand advocacy through experiential marketing, collective consumerism, advocacy patterns, and future shopping trends. Building acquaintance with virtual brands, developing brand communities, and architecting crowd-based branding are the other topics discussed in this chapter.

Thematic Convergence Across Chapters

Thematically, all chapters are interrelated to each other, and this ensures smooth readability, knowledge flow, and maintains topical connectivity and interest. Chapter 1 connects informational updates on the current trends on virtual marketing with Chapter 2 that addresses the diverse challenges in preparing virtual business modeling. As stated earlier, business modeling today is based on seamless technology, and the discussion in Chapter 3 precedes the virtual business modeling perspectives discussed in Chapter 2. Consequently, the thematic discussion flow, information synchronization, and learning interests are well connected across these chapters. The discussion on behavioral perspectives of consumers toward virtual marketing and e-commerce experience have been addressed in Chapter 4 as an impact of virtual marketing practices with focus on hybridity, paradigm shift in shopping practices, and immersive experience. Chapter 4 has been developed to address the effects of virtual marketing to evaluate and justify the virtual trend in business that is inevitably shaping the future market patterns. Virtual branding has been discussed in the last leg of thematic conversation in the book in Chapter 5. Though it is independent discussion, it intrinsically connects to Chapter 2 on virtual business modeling. The last chapter, therefore, discusses strategies to inculcate acquaintances with virtual brands, innovative brand design thinking, and brand architecture. To improve stakeholder engagement in virtual business modeling and innovative brand design thinking, Chapter 5 bridges the discussion with Chapter 2 on crowd-based branding approaches. Stakeholder engagement in virtual marketing benefits the multistake business model and strengthens multistakeholder mechanism in business governance by codesigning the organizational structures, processes, and principles (Shi 2021). In addition, crowdsourcing, crowdfunding, social marketing, and shared economy platforms have been rapidly transforming the production and consumption systems in the developing economies. These platforms connect businesses with economic, social, and environmental factors across geodemographic segments (Mont et al. 2020).

Discussions across chapters streamline the future of shopping using technology and collective consumerism. Growing technology-based retailers like Amazon (VR kiosks), Alibaba (Buy + mobile VR platform), eBay (VR Department Store app), and IKEA (virtual reality kitchen showroom) have been making efforts to embed VR into their e-commerce services as a tool to drive relationship marketing and proximity effects. These firms are trying to transform the future of the shopping ecosystem through head-mounted displays, haptic devices, body-tracking sensors, and motion-tracked controllers to structure future shopping and smart (omnichannel) retailing ecosystem (Xi and Hamari 2021). This chapter also includes a case study on institutional consumer advocacy. The concept of proximity marketing has been explained in context to the various ecosystems and the concept of strategy spinning that affect the business orientation, customer acquisition and loyalty, and market competitiveness of firms. Consequently, business, social, crowd, and behavioral ecosystems significantly contribute to the attributes of virtual marketing. The emerging concepts like profit with purpose and coevolution of business designs are discussed in this book as the core themes of inclusive business that are being practiced by most customer-centric multinational companies. Inclusive business approach overrides the conventional wisdom of leader-centric management practices and is driven by integrative thinking. The new e-commerce business philosophy of inclusive business plays a vital role in integrating people in business processes. It can be achieved by breaking the managerial stigma of *tough-mindedness* (competitive and profit oriented) and moving toward *agile-mindedness* to ensure value-centric business management practices are adopted (Martin and Moldoveanu 2008).

Contribution of the Book

This book discusses the socialization of business as a corporate philosophy to understand customers and stakeholders to motivate the cocreation of value-based business performance through interpersonal experience, values, cognitive reasoning, and interactive communication. Reviewing a wide range of literature from empirical research studies to best practices followed by the companies, this book analyzes the emerging theories of communications, social learning, distinctiveness, corporate social responsibility, social learning, and value cocreation. The concepts and models developed in the book are central to the involvement and engagement of people in business with the increase in socially responsive behavior of companies to support coevolution of business with customers and stakeholders. Thematically, the discussion on these perspectives is interpreted as proximity philosophy in business with multilayered marketing strategies across various geodemographic segments. The focus of the discussion on proximity marketing approaches is precisely on using collective intelligence and collective performance through social networks, interactive communication, and crowd consciousness. This book deliberates upon critical success factors of firms, which include diversity and cross-functionality by managing the triple and quadruple bottom line. It is argued that a timely deployment of streamlined crowd-based marketing strategies in chaotic markets could enhance the effects of social innovation, increase in value-spread among consumers, and reduce growing complexities in global and regional markets. Collective intelligence creates intrinsic and extrinsic motivation with distinctive effects on prosocial behavior, which helps firms understand the effects of crowd behavior

(Festré and Garrouste 2015). This book presents new insights on developing inclusive BMs using both aggressive (crowd-driven) and defensive (competitive) marketing strategies in proximity-driven BMs. The book guides managers on both marketing tactics and marketing strategies using the 5Ts concept for managing Time (first-mover advantage), Territory (new market segments), Target (potential consumers), Thrust (competitive), and Tasks (cocreation).

This book presents contemporary perspectives on virtual marketing with a focus on B-to-C and B-to-B marketing practices. Innovative technology-led e-commerce strategies have been addressed with global best practices and case studies in emerging markets. Case studies are discussed in each chapter to support discussions on various aspects of virtual marketing. Each chapter is provided with an overview of discussions at the beginning and a summary at the end. The visual map of concepts and strategies on inclusive business is supported by creative illustrations and appropriate data in each chapter. Such illustrations make this book appealing to readers and offer smooth transition in learning. This book bridges the new concepts and applications of virtual marketing practices by linking innovation and technology, e-commerce practices, market competition, and customer value in managing multilayered marketing paradigms to achieve long-term business performance. This book specifically discusses the following attributes of virtual businesses in building effective BMs:

- Converging virtual marketing practices with new technology platforms to reduce whiplashes with the cyber–physical marketing matrix,
- Virtual marketing ecosystem and customer engagement to strengthen e-commerce foundation,
- Strategies of growing firms as competitive techniques to gain advantage to build "value-defensive" virtual marketing models,
- Planning technology infrastructure, cybersecurity measures, and strategies to develop interactive value-led business experience in e-commerce, and
- Developing collective engagement in virtual business settings to improve virtual marketing performance across the cyber–physical space.

This book argues that companies need to understand about achieving an inner analytic edge to improve virtual marketing competitiveness and enhance value-driven business in the cyber–physical space. As companies draw competition-based decisions through technology-based e-commerce performance dashboards, this book reviews logical framework analysis and consumer-centered strategies for making sustainable decisions. Customer engagement has emerged as a core concept in developing marketing strategies, though significant research on inclusive business in the context of emotion–decision equilibrium has been limited (Kleinaltenkamp et al. 2019). The book argues that companies need to consider cost-effective technology-led BMs by implementing applied marketing decisions and putting the consumer first in the business management process.

The Audience

The principal audience of this book includes managers, researchers, and students of marketing strategy, marketing research, consumer behavior, and courses on relationship marketing. This book has been developed also to serve as a managerial guide and think-tank for graduate students engaged in studying courses on business strategy and marketing. Besides serving as a reference book to students, this would also be an inspiring book for managers, market analysts, and business consultants engaged in decision-making processes for developing marketing strategy.

The book delineates the need for companies to understand about achieving a technological edge to compete within the hybrid market segment and value-driven customer engagement to augment the market share. Though companies draw some competition-based decisions through technology-based applications and user-friendly interactive platforms and dashboards, the book reviews logical framework analysis and consumer-centered strategies for making technology-led competitive marketing decisions. Customer engagement has emerged as a core concept in developing marketing strategies, though significant research on inclusive business in the context of emotion–decision equilibrium has been limited (Kleinaltenkamp et al. 2019). The book argues that companies need to consider a broader value perspective to enhance the effectiveness of BMs by implementing applied marketing decisions and putting the consumer first in the business management process.

This book will contribute to the existing literature and deliver new concepts to students and researchers alike to pursue the subject further. The book may help working managers find ways to converge best practices with corporate strategies in managing business at destination markets and help students learn new dimensions of marketing strategies.

—Rajagopal

Mexico City

January 15, 2025

References

Alan Stainer, L. S. 1998. "Business Performance: A Stakeholder Approach." *International Journal of Business Performance and Management* 1 (1): 2–12.

Carayannis, E. G. 1999. "Fostering Synergies Between Information Technology and Managerial and Organizational Cognition: The Role of Knowledge Management." *Technovation* 19 (4): 219–31.

Coombs, C., D. Hislop, S. K. Taneva, and S. Barnard. 2020. "The Strategic Impacts of Intelligent Automation for Knowledge and Service Work: An Interdisciplinary Review." *Journal of Strategic Information Systems* 29 (4): 1–30.

de Regt, A., K. Plangger, and S. J. Barnes. 2021. "Virtual Reality Marketing and Customer Advocacy: Transforming Experiences from Story-Telling to Story-Doing." *Journal of Business Research* 136: 513–22.

Desai, H. P. 2014. "Business Models for Inclusiveness." *Procedia—Social and Behavioral Sciences* 157: 353–62.

Farshid, M., J. Paschen, T. Eriksson, and J. Kietzmann. 2018. "Go Boldly! Explore Augmented Reality (AR), Virtual Reality (VR), and Mixed Reality (MR) for Business." *Business Horizons* 61 (5): 657–63.

Fauville, G., A. C. Muller Queiroz, and J. N. Bailenson. 2020. *Virtual Reality as a Promising Tool to Promote Climate Change Awareness*, edited by J. Kim and H. Song. Cambridge, MA: Technology and Health. Academic Press.

Festré, A., and P. Garrouste. 2015. "Theory and Evidence in Psychology and Economics About Motivation Crowding Out: A Possible Convergence?" *Journal of Economic Survey* 29 (2): 339–56.

Fügener, A., J. Grahl, A. Gupta, and W. Ketter. 2021. "Will Humans-in-the-Loop Become Borgs? Merits and Pitfalls of Working with AI." *MIS Quarterly* 45 (3): 1527–56.

Gilboa, S., T. Seger-Guttmann, and O. Mimran. 2019. "The Unique Role of Relationship Marketing in Small Businesses' Customer Experience." *Journal of Retailing and Consumer Services* 51: 152–64.

Helfat, E., and J. A. Martin. 2015. "Dynamic Managerial Capabilities: Review and Assessment of Managerial Impact on Strategic Change." *Journal of Management* 41 (5): 1281–312.

Jingyao, M., Z. Gang, and Z. Ling. 2022. "Governance Mechanisms Implementation in the Evolution of Digital Platforms: A Case Study of the Internet of Things Platform." *R&D Management* 52 (3): 498–516.

Jokinen, L., I. Puumalainen, and M. Airaksinen. 2019. "Influence of Strategic Planning on Product Marketing and Health Service Orientation of Community Pharmacies—A National Survey in Finland." *Health Policy* 123 (5): 462–7.

Jolink, A., and E. Niesten. 2021. "Virtual Reality and Sustainable Behavior in Business." *Cleaner and Responsible Consumption* 2: 100012. https://doi.org/10.1016/j.clrc.2021.100012.

Juntunen, M., E. Ismagilova, and E. L. Oikarinen. 2019. "B2B Brands on Twitter: Engaging Users with a Varying Combination of Social Media Content Objectives, Strategies, and Tactics." *Industrial Marketing Management* 89: 630–41.

Jussupow, E., K. Spohrer, A. Heinzl, and J. Gawlitza. 2021. "Augmenting Medical Diagnosis Decisions? An Investigation into Physicians' Decision-Making Process with Artificial Intelligence." *Information Systems Research* 32 (3): 713–35.

Kane, G. C., R. G. Fichman, J. Gallaugher, and J. Glaser. 2009. "Community Relations 2.0." *Harvard Business Review* 87 (11): 45–50.

Kang, H. J., J. H. Shin, and K. Ponto. 2020. "How 3D Virtual Reality Stores Can Shape Consumer Purchase Decisions: The Roles of Informativeness and Playfulness." *Journal of Interactive Marketing* 49: 70–85.

Kietzmann, J. H. 2017. "Crowdsourcing: A Revised Definition and an Introduction to New Research." *Business Horizons* 60 (2): 151–3.

Kleinaltenkamp, M., I. O. Karpen, C. Plewa, E. Jaakkola, and J. Conduit. 2019. "Collective Engagement in Organizational Settings." *Industrial Marketing Management* 80 (1): 11–23.

Livingston, B. A., and T. R. Opie. 2019. *Even at "Inclusive" Companies, Women of Color Don't Feel Supported.* Harvard Business Review Digital Article. Cambridge, MA: Harvard Business School Press.

Lord, M. D., S. W. Mandel, and J. D. Wager. 2002. "Spinning out a Star." *Harvard Business Review* 80 (6): 115–21.

Maljers, F. A. 1992. "Inside Unilever: The Evolving Transnational Company." *Harvard Business Review* 70 (5): 46–52.

Mancuso, I., A. M. Petruzzelli, and U. Panniello. 2023. "Digital Business Model Innovation in Metaverse: How to Approach Virtual Economy Opportunities." *Information Processing & Management* 60 (5): 103457. https://doi.org/10.1016/j.ipm.2023.103457.

Martin, R., and M. C. Moldoveanu. 2008. *The Future of the MBA: Designing the Thinker of the Future.* Oxford University Press.

Mason, K., and S. Leek. 2012. "Communication Practices in a Business Relationship: Creating, Relating, and Adapting Communication Artifacts Through Time." *Industrial Marketing Management* 41 (2): 319–32.

Melumad, S., R. Hadi, C. Hildebrand, and A. F. Ward. 2020. "Technology-Augmented Choice: How Digital Innovations Are Transforming Consumer Decision Processes." *Customer Needs and Solutions* 7: 90–101.

Mont, O., Y. V. Palgan, K. Bradley, and L. Zvolska. 2020. "A Decade of the Sharing Economy: Concepts, Users, Business and Governance Perspectives." *Journal of Cleaner Production* 269: 122215.https://doi.org/10.1016/j.jclepro.2020.122215.

Muller, E., and R. Peres. 2019. "The Effect of Social Networks Structure on Innovation Performance: A Review and Directions for Research." *International Journal of Research in Marketing* 36 (1): 3–19.

Rajagopal. 2011. "The Symphony Paradigm: Strategy for Managing Market Competition." *Journal of Transnational Management* 16 (3): 181–99.

Rajagopal. 2021. *The Business Design Cube: Converging Markets, Society, and Customer Values to Grow Competitive in Business.* New York: Business Expert Press.

Scheibehenne, B., R. Greifeneder, and P. M. Todd. 2010. "Can There Ever Be Too Many Options? A Meta-Analytic Review of Choice Overload." *Journal of Consumer Research* 37 (3): 409–25.

Schultz, F., S. Utz, and A. Göritz. 2011. "Is the Medium the Message? Perceptions of and Reactions to Crisis Communication via Twitter, Blogs, and Traditional Media." *Public Relationship Review* 37 (1): 20–7.

Shi, H. 2021. "The Application of Social Psychology and Collective Internet Governance." *Aggression and Violent Behavior* 2021: 101588. https://doi.org/10.1016/j.avb.2021.101588.

Spaulding, T. J. 2010. "How Can Virtual Communities Create Value for Business?" *Electronic Commerce Research and Applications* 9 (1): 38–49.

Stokel-Walker, C., and R. Van Noorden. 2023. "What ChatGPT and Generative AI Mean for Science." *Nature* 614: 214–6.

Sturm, T., L. Pumplun, J. P. Gerlach, M. Kowalczyk, and P. Buxmann. 2023. "Machine Learning Advice in Managerial Decision-Making: The Overlooked Role of Decision Makers' Advice Utilization." *Journal of Strategic Information Systems* 32 (4): 101790. https://doi.org/10.1016/j.jsis.2023.101790.

Tiwary, N. K., R. K. Kumar, S. Sarraf, P. Kumar, and N. P. Rana. 2021. "Impact Assessment of Social Media Usage in B2B Marketing: A Review of the Literature and a Way Forward." *Journal of Business Research* 131: 121–39.

Wang, S., R. A. Noe, and Z. Wang. 2014. "Motivating Knowledge Sharing in Knowledge Management Systems." *Journal of Management* 40 (4): 978–1009.

Weech, S., S. Kenny, and M. Barnett-Cowan. 2019. "Presence and Cybersickness in Virtual Reality Are Negatively Related: A Review." *Frontiers in Psychology* 10: 158.

Wei, W., R. Qi, and L. Zhang. 2019. "Effects of Virtual Reality on Theme Park Visitors' Experience and Behaviors: A Presence Perspective." *Tourism Management* 71: 282–93.

Xi, N., and J. Hamari. 2021. "Shopping in Virtual Reality: A Literature Review and Future Agenda." *Journal of Business Research* 134: 37–58.

Zhu, H., Z. Chen, and S. Liu. 2023. "Learning Knowledge Representation with Meta Knowledge Distillation for Single Image Super-Resolution." *Journal of Visual Communication and Image Representation* 95: 103874. https://doi.org/10.1016/j.jvcir.2023.103874.

Acknowledgments

Proximity marketing has been a contemporary topic that has evolved as a potential marketing approach to be explored while I was teaching courses on e-commerce management, and innovation and global competitiveness at Boston University. Proximity marketing has emerged as a promising decision-making domain in the information technology–based strategy platforms of firms. I am thankful to Dr. Tanya Zlateva, dean, Metropolitan College of Boston University, for giving me the opportunity to teach related subjects, which enabled me to apply the research output on sustainability-based business modeling in the classes. Discussions with Dr. Vladimir Zlatev, associate professor of practice at the administrative sciences department, Metropolitan College, Boston University, has also benefited the horizon of knowledge on the subject immensely. Discussions with Dr. Irena Vodenska, department chair, and Dr. Marcus Goncalves, associate chair of the department on this topic also enriched the contents of this book.

I would like to acknowledge the support of Dr. Horacio Arredondo, dean, EGADE Business School, and Dr. Claudia Quintanilla, director, marketing and business intelligence department of EGADE Business School, who have always encouraged me to take up new challenges in teaching graduate courses, develop new insights, and contribute to existing literature prolifically. I thank all my students of graduate and doctoral programs at EGADE Business School for sharing enriching ideas on the subject during classroom discussions, which helped in building this book on the framework of innovative ideas.

I also acknowledge the outstanding support of Scott Isenberg, executive editor of Business Expert Press, who critically examined the proposal, guided the manuscript preparation, and took the publication process forward. I am thankful to various anonymous referees of my previous research works on innovation and technology management who helped me in looking deeper into the conceptual gaps and improving the quality with their valuable comments. Though it was a solo journey with this publication project from ideation to manuscript preparation, I must acknowledge the encouragement from senior academics to proceed ahead with the project. I express my deep gratitude to my wife Arati Rajagopal, who always reminded me of this task over other deadlines on the agenda. She also deserves kudos for copy-editing the manuscript rigorously before submitting it to the publisher.

CHAPTER 1

The Fast Track

Overview

Virtual marketing is emerging out of the transcending evolution of information and communication technology (ICT) widely supported by the AI as one of the major trends in the 21st century. Discussions on fast-track marketing trends based on e-commerce, which has become an embedded practice among B-to-C, B-to-B, hybrid, direct-to-customer (D-to-C), and online-to-offline (O-to-O) retailing firms today using advanced technology platforms is central to this chapter. The current trends in e-commerce are discussed synchronizing the virtual business design using advanced ICT, collective intelligence, and convenience marketing by developing an appropriate technology–business fit. The fast-track development in e-commerce is witnessed in the market, as emerging B-to-C and B-to-B firms are swiftly moving to the virtual space using augmented reality (AR) and virtual reality (VR) devices to push breakthroughs in retailing. This chapter discusses the role of AI, AR, and VR on e-commerce performance, technology-led business modeling, and managing convenience marketing using innovative technology platforms like metaverse.

The rapid advances in information and communication technologies (ICTs) have significantly impacted the digital revolution in business, which has encouraged firms to adapt to automation technologies to improve their manufacturing, logistics, and marketing processes. The technological changes have led to new developments in a number of industries, the retail industry being one of them, which is able to use extensively the technology-based platforms in e-commerce, self-service digital kiosks, social media channels, and general peer interactions. With a series of marketing activities, beginning from ordering the products to check-out, inventory management at stock-keeping units, and developing in-store facilities, retail technology offers innovations and digital solutions in retailing and e-commerce processes. In-store retail technology powered by artificial intelligence (AI) tools such as smart mirrors and self-checkouts plays a pivotal role in generating customer experience. As consumers' engagement with virtual technologies is increasing, both brick-and-mortar and online businesses are increasingly becoming keen on investing in many aspects of retail technology to enhance their business performance. E-commerce businesses have adopted retail technologies that enable efficient inventory management with the cloud software, which enhances the experience in retail operations across multiple platforms.

Virtual Business Scenario

Rapidly growing marketing technology with AI has emerged as a critical factor to gain competitive advantage for both virtual and brick-and-mortar companies engaged in B-to-C and B-to-B marketing segments. The AI-supported marketing technology has significantly attracted consumers to online marketplaces and e-services like meal kit and food delivery, which creates customer value and enhances firm's marketing efficiency. Investment into these segments has grown substantially, encouraging businesses to pursue digital transformation and upgrade transactional platforms with AI-supported tools. Retail technology aids both brick-and-mortar and e-commerce companies in several stages of their business processes. Supply chain and logistics are areas where both online and conventional retail companies benefit from digital solutions. However, e-commerce and multichannel businesses heavily depend on retail technologies today to gain efficiency in payments and personalization. Consequently, investment in retailing is the need of the hour for firms to transform retail venues into experiential spaces.

Transformation of retailing services—such as 360° product views and features, informational touchpoints, interactive displays, and applications for mobile devices—has increased the perceived usefulness of these technology attributes among consumers (Grewal et al. 2017). For example, during the lockdown that was imposed worldwide because of the COVID-19 pandemic, retailers focused on e-commerce as the active transactional channel over existing physical stores. However, the omnichannel approach to retailing remained effective in creating unified experience between brick-and-mortar and online channels, including interactive web stores. Retail technologies are increasingly encouraging customers to gain new experience in comprehending product attributes and such attributes' fit to their needs, value for money, and shopping enjoyment using technology-based self-service. Gen AI has taken all industries by storm, and retail is one of the leading sectors where the application of advanced AI applications can bring many benefits. Areas where retail executives are looking to deploy AI include personalization, supply chain management, and security (Rajagopal 2022).

The integration of digital information with augmented reality (AR) technology synchronizes marketing operations with the physical environment to offer users a real-time experience. Such a blend of technology into conventional computer-aided platforms helps firms to increase customer satisfaction and firms' competitiveness in business operations. AR combines real-life images with a superimposed image or animation using the camera on a mobile device or through AR headsets and glasses by mixing graphics, sounds, haptic feedback, or even smell to the natural world as it exists to provide high satisfaction to users. As part of the wider extended reality (XR), the technology industry has doubled the global AR market size to penetrate the most profitable and visible segments of e-commerce market in both B-to-B and B-to-C market segments. The retail industry market coupled with AX and AR is expected to grow considerably over the years in future. AX is a software of Microsoft for retailing firms, which equips the dynamic retailer to conduct retailing operations across channels locally or globally with the technology and features to connect with customer and key partners, empower customers, and offer the needed insight for initiative-taking execution. Therefore, AX is also referred as Agent Experience used to measure customer experience (CX) as how happy they are with firm's strategy *and* how they are being served. Besides, industrial and retail marketers and firms in consumer-to-consumer (C-to-C) market segments, such as May Kay Cosmetics, Avon, AliExpress, and eBay, have gained popularity in global e-commerce and have driven the market toward mobile users through AI-supported applications. In addition to online platforms on desktop and mobile devices, small e-commerce players and online retailers sell their products via mobile shopping applications as well as social media platforms. The e-commerce industry is fraught with multiple challenges at a time when the global economy is undergoing significant changes as the macroeconomic factors due to politico-economic volatility have been unfavorable to e-commerce companies. In addition, increasing prevalence of AI in virtual retail environment poses challenges for e-commerce retailers in meeting consumer expectations in terms of personalization, self-services efficiency, and cybersecurity to protect personal data.

Global trends of e-commerce have shown that the overall revenue in the global e-commerce segment is projected to reach US$4,117 billion by the end of 2024 and expected to show a compound annual growth rate (CAGR) of 9.49 percent in global e-commerce between 2024 and 2029. This growth is projected to result in a market volume of US$6,478 billion by 2029. Among most countries that have adapted to e-commerce as an emerging technology-led business channel, with a projected market volume of US$1,469 billion in 2024, the largest revenue is generated in China. In the global e-commerce market segment, the number of users is expected to increase by 3.6 billion by 2029. Currently, the user penetration might go up by 40.5 percent at the end of 2024, which is expected to rise as high as 49.1 percent by 2029 while the average revenue per user (ARPU) is expected to reach US$1,620. According to recent industry calculations, Turkey will rank first among 20 countries worldwide in retail e-commerce development between 2024 and 2029, with a CAGR of 11.6 percent. The Turkish e-commerce market is currently valued at 3.4 trillion Turkish lira. India and Brazil are also among the fastest-growing e-commerce markets globally, with CAGRs over 11 percent. The global retail e-commerce CAGR was estimated at 9.5 percent during the same period (Statista, n.d.).

As a result of technological growth, customers now have access to extended information on products and stores by scanning the Quick Response (QR) codes associated with physical products delivered to customers. The scanning of QR codes provides customers with one-touch comprehensive information on products purchased and increases the usefulness of technology, while retailers benefit from reducing the cost and time to share on real-time the product and market information with customer through conventional channels. Retailing technologies that focus on QR, just-in-time, ease-of-use, and direct delivery attract customers to shop with confidence. In addition, customer services provide higher usefulness of retailing technologies and customer satisfaction (Renko and Druzijanic 2014). Retailing technology today has also encouraged customers to redeem their promotional coupons online, which has not only helped in developing customer loyalty to retail organizations or brands but has also helped retailers increase their sales volume. Use of promotional coupons elicits emotions, peer influence, purchase intentions, and repeat-buying behavior among customers. The price-discount factors influence impulsive buying behavior among consumers, and impulsiveness tends to develop positive cognitive enactments. Electronic coupons induce both positive and negative effects depending on the reputation of an online retail company and the fairness of discounts or promotion offered to a specific product. In online retailing, e-coupons are mainly circulated as scratch-code-based coupons, e-mail coupons, and promotional coupons. Price and volume promotions through redemption of coupons involve both planned and impulsive buying behavior. Some studies have revealed that impulsiveness is largely driven by reward-seeking behavior (Rajagopal 2022).

In switching from shopping in physical stores to virtual retail outlets, consumers are gaining a wide range of benefits by embracing virtual retailing technology—such as quick comparisons on price and quality of products, online promotions, and peer motivation on adapting to retailing technology—which augments shopping experience and improves the perceived value of a product and/or the seller. In a physical store, consumers derive motivation through sensory stimuli that reinforce the desire to shop. On the other hand, environmental stimuli are restricted to affecting vision or hearing in an online store. Peer interactions encourage customers to adapt to innovative retailing technologies like AR, quick-response codes to obtain comprehensive product information, self-controlled checkouts, and managing product deliveries. Digital communications through social media channels and blogs of customer communities have emerged today as guiding tools for customers to make online shopping decisions, such as choosing shopping outlets that are less complicated, contain wide product portfolios, and are trustworthy (Lamberton and Stephen 2016).

Virtual stores and e-commerce have grown faster along with transcending ICT. The evolution of e-commerce and the engagement of AI have transformed marketing technology as exhibited in Figure 1.1.

The beginning of the timeline of e-commerce goes back to the 1970s, progressively contributing to global businesses by integrating advances in technology over time. The decennial growth of e-commerce and AI is illustrated in Figure 1.1. E-commerce was initiated in the 1970s through Baxter healthcare modem as an online ordering system for healthcare products. Baxter, a major healthcare and medical products firm, pioneered e-commerce technology and encouraged streamlined ordering and inventory management for hospitals and healthcare providers, which enabled them to connect with Baxter's ordering system via a dedicated modem. This practice encouraged automated inventory management in a real-time environment to update product availability and facilitate automated restocking. It improved supply chain process, data tracking and analytics, and processing of bulk orders by achieving cost-efficiency. This modem-based e-commerce solution was a groundbreaking application of early online ordering technology. During the 1980s, French Mintel System (FMS) was launched as an improvement over the Baxter's modem-based ordering system alongside the standardization of electronic data exchange (EDI) protocol. FMS was developed by the state-owned French telecommunication company, which provided digital services over the telephone to a widely dispersed and far-located geodemographic population. The FMS provided an online directory with services portals that could be accessed by users through a small terminal-like device connecting users for online transactions on a large scale. French businesses recognized the potential to expand their business through FMS—with FMS users could do online banking transactions, book train and airline tickets, payment processing, and enjoy home delivery services. FMS users used to pay service charges for per-minute usage of the system through their phone bills. Advertisements and promotions were also placed online by businesses successfully using the FMS, which has significantly influenced the growth of modern e-commerce process and served as a model for developing online retail platforms, digital payment systems, and developing early web portals.

Advancement of ICT during the 1990s has encouraged e-commerce with the extended usage of broadband Internet. In this decade, Amazon

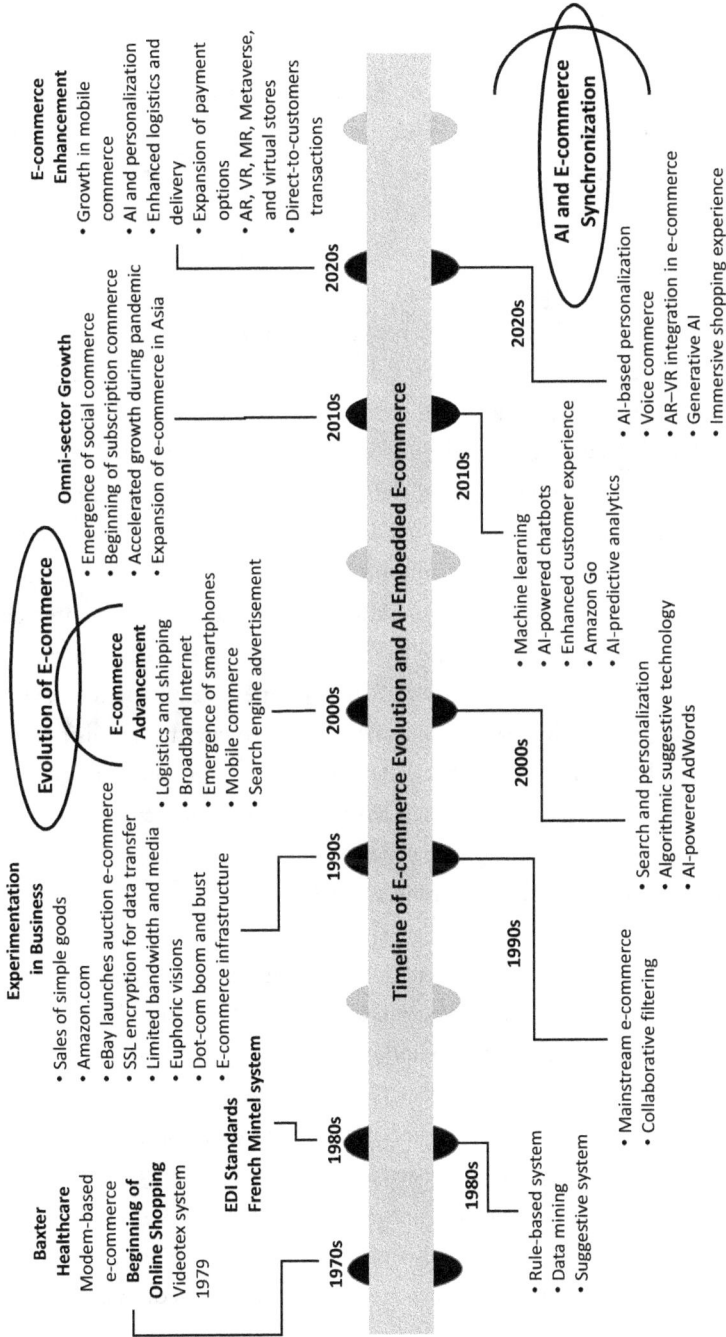

Figure 1.1 Timeline of e-commerce and its engagement with AI

developed illustrative e-commerce for selling consumer products online, while eBay launched an auction-based e-commerce, which offered new experience to consumers in North America and Europe. E-commerce in China began with primitive electronic data exchanges in the early 1990s and rolled out the first online retail transaction in 1998. Alibaba, a leading e-commerce giant, offered an e-commerce platform for online transactions in 1999, initially focusing on business in the industrial (B-to-B) segment. The development of Secure Socket Layers (SSL) technology helped in encrypting the personal information of consumers and data transfer process, which strengthened the e-commerce transactions and user confidence in carrying out online operations. The popularity of e-commerce triggered the boom-and-bust of Dot.com businesses during the 1990s.E-commerce significantly advanced during the 2000s decennium and reinforced the shipping and logistics operations to ensure timely delivery of orders and enhance customer satisfaction (see Figure 1.1). The proximity of broadband Internet in developed countries and big emerging markets has increased manifold, which facilitated e-commerce businesses to grow fast and securely. The mobile commerce has also grown in this decade with increasing use of smartphones. Search engine advertisements have made headway globally to push e-commerce businesses' growth to be at par with the brick-and-mortar business segment.

The following decade of 2010s has witnessed omni-sector growth in e-commerce with the emergence of social commerce linking social media platforms like Facebook, Instagram, and TikTok to businesses, facilitating buying and selling operations. Social marketing, a form of online business practice, has significantly enhanced consumer experience, user engagement, influencers' collaboration, and personalization of buying and selling processes. During this period, the subscription business model, as one of the streams of e-commerce, has flourished worldwide, in which customers pay a recurring fee to receive products or services on a regular basis. This model helped businesses to maintain customer loyalty and a steady cash flow. E-commerce has experienced precipitous growth during the COVID-19 business shutdown in most parts of the world, which has driven many brick-and-mortar companies to switch to e-commerce. Most customer-centric businesses later maintained both online and physical stores as hybrid BMs. The current decade of 2020s has witnessed steady growth in mobile commerce and use of AI in e-commerce. Enhanced use of AI has helped e-commerce firms manage customer support, logistics, and improve and maintain efficiency in order delivery. The varied benefits of AI have emerged, such as new devices of AR, VR, and mixed reality. The metaverse, a shared virtual business experience, has also been introduced at the beginning of this decade. The metaverse is a collective virtual shared space, created by the convergence of virtually enhanced physical and digital realities. It is often described as the next iteration of the Internet, where users, represented by avatars, can interact in immersive 3D environments. Toward the latter part of the decade, the concept of the metaverse emerged, with retailers experimenting with virtual stores and digital goods. Brands like Nike, Gucci, and others created virtual spaces where users could explore products and make purchases within immersive environments, potentially using cryptocurrency or digital tokens.

Synchronization of AI with virtual businesses has transformed e-commerce gradually over the decades as presented in Figure 1.1. The AI support had appeared in the 1980s with the rule-based system in inventory management and logistics. The system supported repetitive tasks with limited agility in operations. AI also supported data-mining analytics to help business firms analyze buying data and associated customer insights. Amazon introduced the first AI-based suggestive system using collaborative filtering to analyze the buying history of consumers and update their profiles accordingly. In the early 2000s, AI-driven recommendation systems became sophisticated in integrating complex data analytics. The AI-powered AdWords initiated by Google has transformed digital advertising, which helped e-commerce businesses to reach customers through automated bidding and keywords optimization. During the 2010s, machine learning and chatbots have contributed to the growth of e-commerce to enhance consumer experience. Advances in machine learning allowed AI to process larger datasets. Personalization algorithms began leveraging comprehensive data to customize shopping experiences during this decade. Increasing use of AI has driven chatbot technology to surge ahead, with brands using AI-powered bots on websites and social media to handle customer inquiries and provide uninterrupted service. At the end of 2010s, AI-driven predictive analytics allowed e-commerce platforms to anticipate demand and manage inventory better, optimizing stock levels based on sales forecasts. Facilitating the features of AI, *Amazon Go*, a chain of convenience stores operated by Amazon, was launched in early 2018, and it offers a unique shopping experience without traditional checkouts or cashiers with the *just-walk-out technology*. In this technology shopping bid, customers enter the store by scanning a QR code from the Amazon Go app at the entrance. The store uses a combination of computer vision, sensor fusion, and deep learning algorithms to track items that customers pick up and put in their virtual cart. Completing the sales, customers walk out of the store, and the Amazon account of customers is automatically charged.

The salient contribution of AI to e-commerce during the 2020s, including AI-enabled personalization, reached new heights with companies using real-time data to tailor experiences across platforms from suggestive to dynamic pricing, *Voice Commerce*, and AR tools, and these tools have gained immense popularity. These attributes of e-commerce are supported with AI-driven tools providing unique services such as product visualizations, interactive shopping, and virtual try-ons. In the same period, generative AI became popular for creating content by allowing e-commerce businesses to use AI to generate product descriptions, which significantly helped firms to enhance customer support responses and refine personalization. The integration of AI with advanced augmented/virtual reality (AR/VR) and the metaverse allowed for immersive shopping experiences, where AI curates personalized product showrooms and virtual assistants that guide users.

The usefulness of retail technologies is perceived to be highly informative in the context of website layout, quality of information, and user-generated content on products and services. Most websites consist of product pictures, videos, and interactive tools to augment product usage with complementary text descriptions and increase the scope of product recognition among customers. Retail websites with colorful layouts, categorical arrays of products, back-and-forth navigation with retention of previous searches, interactive tools, and online chat rooms are perceived by customers as quality online platforms, which may make the shopping navigation interesting and reduce the stress in product search among customers. The quality of retailing websites, therefore, integrates usefulness of retailing technologies, impulsive buying, and deriving value for money among customers (Rajagopal 2022). AR is one of the interactive technologies that enhances consumer emotions and perceptions and develops cognitive ergonomics. AR influences anthropomorphic feelings of consumers and contributes to retail anthropomorphism. To complement the AR experience, retail firms have adopted chatbots to interact with consumers through various communication channels, including social media, live chat, and SMS (short messaging services). In addition, digital networks support conversational commerce that helps companies to not only support customers in product selection but also broaden their choices throughout the shopping and decision-making processes (Leung and Yan-Chan 2020).

Technology Trends in Marketing

The e-commerce market is growing exponentially with dynamic technology, which has exhibited six trends that heavily impacted the global market. Among many technology-led marketing trends, the principal technology interventions that have significantly affected marketing practices include AI, AR, live commerce, online-to-offline (O-to-O) e-commerce, social commerce, and voice assistants. The recent technology development has introduced generative AI in marketing operations among firms engaged in the B-to-C, B-to-B, hybrid, and D-to-C segments has opened up greater opportunities for value-creating personalization among consumers, using dynamic pricing, developing user-friendly chatbots, creating voice- and virtual assistants, and improving customer search options to enhance the proximity of market to both existing and new geodemographic consumer segments. Digital networking, social media, and virtual consumer engagements in building and serving online customer relationships have significantly encouraged social commerce, a form of e-commerce in which a social media platform serves as both a marketing channel and a shopping destination. Social commerce is expected to grow by more than 50 percent between 2021 and 2025. The major trends in e-commerce today include the following attributes:

- Business trends
  - Retail e-commerce, m-commerce, and on-demand services

- Technology trends
  - Mobile platform and cloud computing
  - Big data
    - Structured, semi-structured, and unstructured data
    - Collected by organizations
    - Data mining, predictive projects, advanced analytical applications
  - Internet of Things
    - Collective network of connected devices
    - Cloud communication
- Societal trends
- Increased concern about impact of social networks
- Concerns about increasing market dominance of big technology firms.

Among changing technology-led business trends, e-commerce and m-commerce have emerged as major technology aids. M-commerce, or mobile commerce, is one of the emerging practices of buying and selling goods and services using a wireless device like a smartphone or a tablet. It is a type of e-commerce that allows users to shop online using only a mobile communication device and without a desktop computer. The changing technological trends exhibit popular user practices on mobile platforms or cloud-based applications. Cloud computing is the on-demand availability of computing resources, including storage, servers, and software, over the Internet without physical resources. The growth of the concept of Big Data has encouraged industrial firms to make use of data to make real-time decisions on vital business indicators like pricing, logistics and supply chain, and demand-and-supply articulations. Big Data can be described as a collection of data that help e-commerce businesses improve their performance and gain a competitive advantage. It helps in personalizing the shopping experience by providing behavior-specific recommendations to both customers and firms and increases the visibility of product information. Big Data also improves the decision-making abilities of firms to optimize production, logistics, and marketing strategies by providing tailor-made data-based analytical information to develop appropriate strategies that could fit consumer's needs. Data-mining results, predictive measures, and advanced analytical applications are often derived through Big Data. Another significant trend that has emerged in the market is Internet of Things (IoT), which refers to the collective network of connected devices that facilitate and establish communication between devices and the cloud, as well as between the devices themselves. It is basically a network of physical devices, vehicles, appliances, and other physical objects that are embedded with sensors, software, and network connectivity that allow the connected devises and platforms to collect and share data. The IoT devices have a broad range of applications, from establishing connectivity with simple "smart home" devices like smart thermostats, to wearables like smartwatches and radio frequency identification (RFID)-enabled clothing, to complex industrial machinery and transportation systems.

The e-commerce market has grown exponentially since the beginning of the 21st century. The conventional market ecosystem has transformed itself into a web of technology-led BMs with the advancement of AI-boosted transaction platforms pushing new e-commerce trends in all business segments. The rate of digital adoption has doubled across countries, which suggests online retail might be responsible for half of all retail revenues by the end of 2030. Moreover, in general, firms are expanding their business on the competitive digital footprint and placing more emphasis on hybrid stores. However, over time, it has been witnessed that technology-based market applications have high saturation in the market. An electronics or home goods retailer now competes globally, not just with its direct competitors but also with small-scale online stores and e-commerce giants like Amazon. This can force businesses to drastically bring down prices to compete, and this might disrupt customer value.

In the constantly shifting, rapidly expanding e-commerce ecosystem, businesses are able to grow creatively with their digital strategies for creating dynamic, interactive shopping experiences that aim to improve customer relationships. Amidst the massive shifts in technology-driven marketing practices, the consumers today purchase goods and services in an digital environment that enhance a customer's digital shopping experience through the following technological advancements:

- AI
- AR

- VR
- Mixed reality
- CRM Chatbots
- Online-to-offline e-commerce
- Social commerce
- Voice assistants
- Metaverse business

Consumers today are used to shopping online and tracking same-day delivery of customized products, expecting a seamless and unified digital shopping experience. Shipping and logistics have become easy and encouraging through technology intervention in new markets and are subject to global supply chain efficiency. Increasingly, customers desire benefits like free shipping or designated loyalty programs. Successful markets are digitally embedded with native demographics like Gen Z, and businesses demonstrate a commitment to sustainability. The growth in marketing technology has various implications for marketing efficiency as exhibited in Figure 1.2.

Radical technological trends have emerged with the extensive use of AI and ML that have significantly driven the *Industry 5.0* revolution on automation of production and business operations in the 21st century. Figure 1.2 exhibits technological augmentations that support data-based decisions, automation, and cloud applications. Broadly, marketing technology includes integration of AI and machine learning. In addition, technologies like AR, VR, and mixed reality along with the IoT combine several Internet-based devices to enable more effective and closer monitoring and control of transactions. The global marketing technology market was valued at approximately $325.7 billion in 2022 and is expected to grow at a compound annual growth rate (CAGR) of 19.8 percent between 2023 and 2030; this has attracted heavy investment by both technology firms and business firms in this segment. The underlying objective for investing in marketing technology is to enhance marketing capabilities and improve customer engagement in business processes, transactions, and value cocreation (Grand View Research 2024).

One of the major contributions of technology in enhancing the marketing performance of consumer-centric firms is driving the business to

Cloud environment
Information storage
Data sharing
Resource pooling

AI and
collective
intelligence

Artificial Intelligence
Generative AI
Predictive AI

Crowd
Cloud
Confidence

- Digital representation
- Blockchain operations
- Virtual assets market
- Immersive experience

Metaverse Technology

- Connectivity across devices
- Scalability in business
- Automation and control
- Cybersecurity and monitoring

Machine Learning

Internet of Things

Mixed Reality

- Physical and digital blend
- Real-time interaction
- Collaborative capabilities
- Human–computer interface

**Virtual
Reality**

- Immersion
- Sensory feedback
- 3D visualization
- Motion tracking
- Spatial audio

- Data-driven decision
- Data-pattern mapping
- Automation of processes
- Fraud detection and surveillance

**Augmented
Reality**

Growth in Marketing Technology

- Combination of real
  and virtual world
- Real-time interaction
- 3D Object tracking
- Geolocation
- Smart glass support
- SLAM technology
- Cloud storage

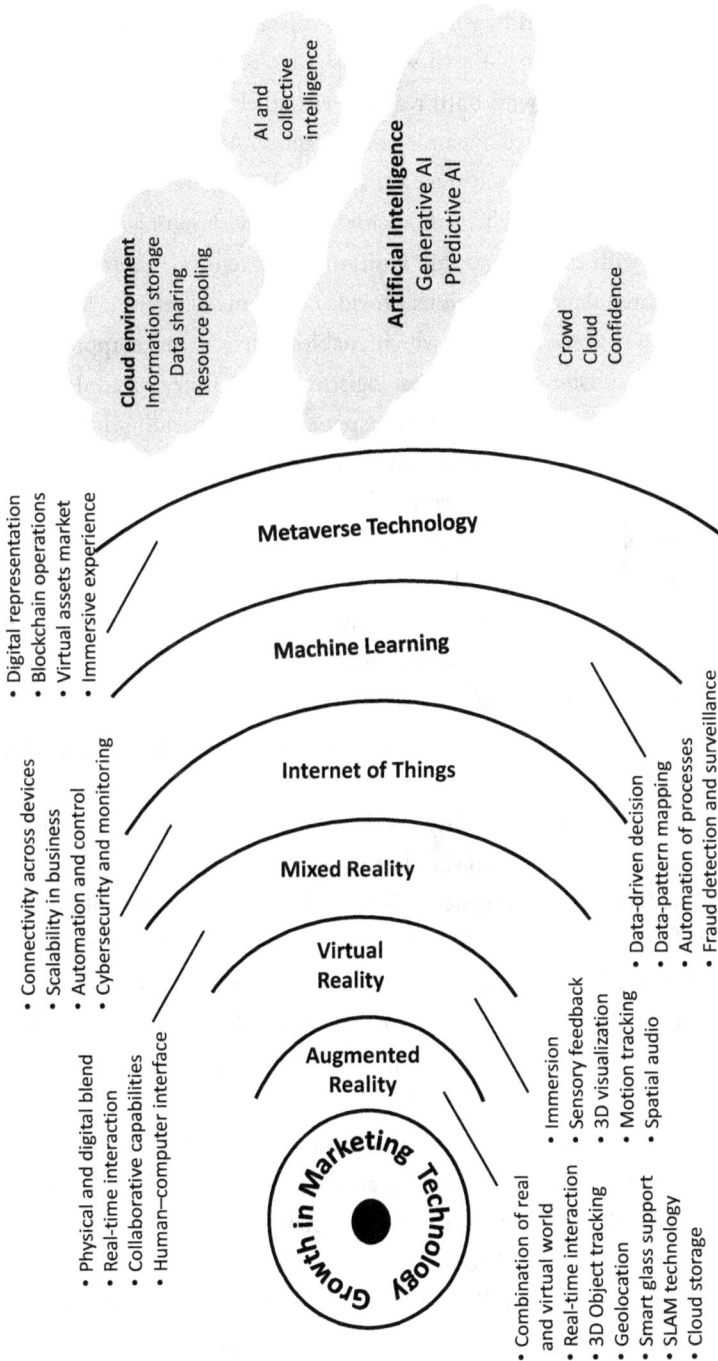

Figure 1.2 Technology in marketing and decision-making

use the benefits of AR as illustrated in Figure 1.2. AR is a combination of real and virtual worlds, which overlays digital content onto the physical world by blending the two seamlessly. Users experiencing AR with headsets can interact with both real and virtual elements simultaneously to make their experience dynamic and engaging. AR provides 3D object tracking, as AR systems can trace the path and integrate 3D objects into the user's environment, which allows for immersive shopping experiences. Combined with the Geographic Positioning System (GPS) and remote location–based data, AI solutions provide contextually relevant information based on user's location, which enables firms to make appropriate decisions on consumer preferences, logistics, and delivery schedules. Devices like smart glasses enhance AR experiences by providing hands-free interaction and more immersive visuals, while the Simultaneous Localization and Mapping (SLAM) technology helps AR systems in mapping the geographic environment and tracking the user's position within it, improving the accuracy and quality of interactions between users and sellers. Such contribution of AR has helped firms to improve live communication with consumers, to provide them with real-time and geographic-oriented solutions and cocreate value in business. Cloud storage enables AR applications to store and retrieve data from the cloud providing complex but data-rich experiences.

Unlike AR, virtual reality (VR) creates immersive, computer-generated environments that simulate real or fantasy objects within a chosen or predetermined ambience. VR provides a sense of being physically present in a nonphysical world, through headsets and other devices that block out the real world and replace it with a virtual one. Users interact with virtual environment in real-time, manipulating objects, navigating spaces, and experiencing changes in the environment based on their actions as the 3D environment of VR provides depth and realism that make the experience more convincing through high-quality graphics. Advanced VR systems track users' movements and adjust the virtual environment accordingly. This includes head tracking, hand tracking, and even full-body tracking with spatial audio features based on user's position and orientation, adding to the realism of the experience. Brick-and-mortar firms use VR to promote gaming and entertainment products, as these features make VR a powerful tool not only to create consumer value but also to drive impulsive purchase intentions and buying decisions. Mixed Reality (MXR) combines elements of both the physical and digital subjects and ambience by creating an environment where real and virtual objects can interact seamlessly. This technology integrates real-world and computer-generated elements, allowing them to coexist and interact in real-time. One of the salient features of MXR is the collaboration capability, which allows multiple users to interact within the same virtual environment facilitating individual or team collaboration and sharing of experiences. These attributes make MXR a versatile and powerful technology with applications across various fields, from fashion and entertainment to education and healthcare and industrial design.

The Internet of Things (IoT) is another milestone in technological growth, which has significantly affected product market, industry, and quality and lifestyle of users, as it connects physical devices to the Internet, allowing both product/service providers and users to collect and exchange data to help establish a closer and more efficient monitoring and control of processes. IoT devices are connected to the Internet to enable communication between devices and systems. It can also be scaled up to accommodate a large number of devices, making it suitable for various applications from small homes to large industrial setups. IoT enables automation of processes and remote-controlling of devices, improving efficiency and reducing the need for manual intervention. However, ensuring the security of IoT devices and the data they generate is critical, involving measures like encryption and access controls. Another stage of technological growth along with extensive applications of AI is machine learning, which largely supports data-based decisions in business and industry. Machine learning relies heavily on data. The more data it has, the better it can learn and make accurate predictions and can, using algorithms, detect patterns in large datasets, which helps in making predictions. In addition, machine learning helps firms to automate complex tasks that would be difficult or time-consuming for humans to perform.

Metaverse is the recent technological drive for businesses that tend to operate totally virtually. It is an evolving digital universe that blends virtual (VR) and augmented (AR) realities to create immersive experiences. An immersive experience can be defined as a neurobehavioral feel that engages the senses, making participants feel as though they are part of the event or environment rather than just observers. This can be achieved through various technologies and methods, creating a sense of presence and involvement. In metaverse, users can create digital representations of themselves, which can be customized to reflect their real-life appearance or something entirely unique. Metaverse has opened a virtual assets market, where users can buy, sell, and trade virtual real estate, which is often represented as non-fungible tokens.

In the recent past, *live commerce experience* has been unveiled to customers in China. This technology platform that emerged in 2016 brought US$647 billion into the country. The e-commerce giant Alibaba launched Taobao Live, popularizing live shopping in China. The livestream landscape is much more fragmented in the United States, but even as shoppers return to stores, retailers and large technology firms are betting that consumers will continue searching for and purchasing items on their phones. Live commerce in the United States is growing and forecasted to gain around US$32 billion at the end of 2023. During live commerce events, customers are able to interact with a host over a live stream to purchase products by using digital wallets in a real-time environment. This sales approach to support e-commerce performance has been introduced by the Chinese social media network Alibaba. Later the concept of live commerce has been adopted by online retail businesses like TikTok, Amazon, and clothing resale platforms like Poshmark. During shopping events, influencers and celebrities are encouraged or sponsored to promote brands, encouraging consumers to discuss the products on offer and their eventual sale through social media. Using live commerce, businesses promote their brands encouraging a sense of companionship and solidarity with the brand in a specific event. During 2022, Walmart, YouTube, and eBay added or expanded their live shopping features (Holman and Huang 2023).

In 2012, Heineken, a Dutch beermaker, asked designers in different destinations about how the future of nightclubs in Europe should be. Many volunteer product designers, customers, and product critiques joined the campaign, and their semantically mapped opinions were presented at Milan's Design Week in 2012, with a live recreation of the space. Apart from being a cocreation success story, Heineken's cocreation initiative has attracted considerable media impact, and it has also become a reference campaign in terms of advertising and marketing. In addition,

Heineken launched its cocreation platform in 2012, asking game lovers, beer drinkers, and environmentally conscious consumers for ideas that would make its packaging more sustainable. Similarly, Threadless, a fashion e-commerce company that manages and sells crowdsourced T-shirt designs, built a sustainable model by producing high-quality shirts in limited quantities to create the sense of a premium brand. The company pushed cocreation by inviting users to suggest designs and buying preferences. Consumers posted their design on the website while other users voted on the design options, and the creations that received maximum support from the community were produced. Threadless is an artistic creation and has become a profitable business. Crowdsourcing, therefore, raises an evident example of sustainable payoff among large, small, and startup ventures alike (Boghin 2014).

Artificial Intelligence (AI)

Chronologically, AI has evolved since the mid-20th century from a crude form of expert system to the generative AI being experienced today. AI has emerged as a system's ability to interpret external data correctly, learn contents from the data, derive interpretations, use the learnings to disseminate among target, and achieve specific goals/tasks through flexible adaptation to information, processes, and systems. AI was confined to an area of relative scientific obscurity and limited applied scope for over half a century. However, with the emergence of Big Data, computer-aided business solutions, and decision-making abilities, AI has entered the new phase of Industrial Revolution and public conversation. Over time, artificial neural networks have reemerged as form of Deep Learning with AlphaGo, a program developed by Google that was able to beat the world champion in the board game Go and was seen making more sensitive moves than the conventional chessboard game, enabling AI-based challenges in computer–human interfaces. AlphaGo achieved its high performance by using a specific type of artificial neural network called Deep Learning. Today, artificial neural networks and Deep Learning form the basis of most AI applications. They are the basis of image recognition algorithms used by Facebook and speech recognition algorithms that fuel smart speakers and auto-pilot cars (Haenlein and Kaplan 2019).

AI is transiting from Industry 4.0 to Industry 5.0 technology revolution, marking a shift from AI informatics to AI robotics to facilitate marketing processes and create new experiences and high-perceived value among customers. The impact of marketing technology on digital commerce has been immense. Digital optimization and automation tools have proved to be convenient and cost-effective for businesses, as businesses can now use customer data or third-party data by creating intelligent e-commerce sites. Deployed correctly, AI-enabled marketing and product discovery tools can facilitate firms to promote customer engagement and develop plans for acquisition of new customers and retention of existing customers. There are several industrial applications of AI, which include particularly its use as a surveillance tool for operational maintenance and safety. In the United Kingdom, Network Rail utilizes AI to forecast and prevent equipment failures. By analyzing data from sensors placed along the tracks, AI systems can identify signs of wear and tear, or potential malfunctions before they lead to actual failures. This proactive maintenance strategy helps minimize downtime, enhance safety, and ensure that trains operate on schedule. Similarly in the developing counties with high pressure of population on public services, AI has significantly supported industrial operations. Indian Railways is utilizing AI-driven predictive maintenance to oversee the condition of tracks and trains. AI algorithms evaluate data from sensors on locomotives and tracks to anticipate potential failures and schedule maintenance in advance. This approach reduces downtime, enhances safety, and lowers maintenance costs.[1]

THE YES, a multi-brand shopping app was launched in 2020 in the United States, which offered an innovative buying experience for women's fashion. This shopping app has been driven by AI with a complex algorithm, which has been derived from data science research and machine learning. The app aimed to create and deliver a personalized store for every shopper based on shopping preferences, designs and styles, size, and budget. When a woman shopper intended to download THE YES app, it means she embarks on an interactive shopping journey that provides

---

[1]For details see Rail Analysis in India: Gateway to the Rail and Metro Sector in India. Accessed November 11, 2024. https://news.railanalysis.com/article-impact-of-artificial-intelligence-in-railways/.

her the experience of enjoyment, satisfaction, easy shopping process, and, in general, a shopping experience that exceeds the metrics of desired user experience (UX). Similar to many dating apps that collect a stream of personal and body data from women users, the app could be used dynamically to set new preferences and levels of satisfaction. The app company continued with serving the UX factor and improving the algorithmic synchronization with consumer data, preferences, fashion trend, and brands to deliver on the company's customer value proposition. THE YES app also focused on customer acquisition via paid media, with the idea that more users on the app improve the algorithm's performance. The app also synchronized the social shopping features with social media to make the shopping experience more viral and help the brands or firms develop an influencer program to bring fashion influencer voices onto the platform and design customer loyalty program accordingly (Avery et al. 2021).

AI algorithms help in analyzing voluminous customer data, including browsing history, purchasing behavior, and demographic information, to deliver personalized product recommendations and tailored shopping experiences. The AI-based personalization understands consumer behavior through their search history and contextual use of keywords and exhibits goods a consumer is most likely to buy, reminds customers when it's time to refill an order, and offers shopping experiences tailored to an individual's preferences. These personalized shopping experiences can be deployed as key customer touchpoints by earmarking product pages, e-mail campaigns, and wish lists during the checkout process. AI has demonstrated successful contribution to the dynamic pricing used by airlines in passenger ticketing, Uber services, and pricing of accommodation in the hospitality industry, including Airbnb services. The services of AI-powered chatbots are continuously improving, and it is expected that by 2030 they will become the technology providing personalized customer support in natural language, answering questions, and addressing consumer concerns in real-time, which could be used by many organizations across the developing and developed countries. AI-powered search and recommendation engines use machine learning algorithms to better capture user intent, improve search relevance, and enhance product discovery. For example, large retailers are engaging third-party AI (link resides outside of ibm.com) to make searching for products in natural language simpler, so shoppers can search by pattern or style and find the exact item they're looking to buy. The principal attributes of AI-based shopping, advertising, logistics, and other marketing-related platforms are as stated below:

- Ubiquity, omnipresence
- Global reach
- Universal standards
- Information richness
- Interactivity
- Information density
- Personalization, customization
- Social technology
- 3C factors—Crowd, Cloud, and Confidence

AI-powered search engines use machine learning algorithms to better capture user intent, improve search relevance, and enhance product discovery. Large retailers are engaging third-party AI services to make searching for products in natural language simpler, so shoppers can search by pattern or style and find the exact item they're looking to buy. Such AI-based search converges the 3C factors to provide access of information to crowd-based users, holds cloud as the generic large information repository, and tends to create confidence among AI users and consumers about the speed of information retrieval and dissemination and its accuracy and contextual relevance in desired results of AI-based search.

AI in marketing has a new space to grow in customer-centric firms. AI has gone beyond robotics structures for customers, as it is now emerging as a tool for decision-making in consumer-oriented firms. Coding using multiple information and communication technology (ICT) tools has been central to value creation and has provided efficient services for enhancing consumers' experiences. AI can now manage data analysis and deliver managerial decisions to tourism firms. However, the human element is not totally replaced with machines in managing firms. AI is integrated with ICTs to be omnipresent in all stages of a tourist's journey and supports the ecstasy of customers (Buhalis et al. 2019). Early in this century, social robots played a pivotal role in serving the social institutions and, tourism industry in particular, to disseminate information and converse with humans. Broadly, Alexa and Siri are also accommodated as social robots with AI capabilities that can interact with humans. The arrival of Generative AI has ushered in a new era in AI revolution in the public domain to develop interactive relationships and mutual dependency to learn and bridge the information silos. AI robots serve as coworkers and analysts for decision-making in large multi-brand and international customer-centric firms. AI has yet to support tourism and hospitality industry robots with trust, anticipation, and emotions. Happiness, arousal, and merriment have a significant impact on robot sentiment polarity, while anticipation and surprise do not significantly affect AI logarithms. Therefore, one major challenge is to anthropomorphize robots for tourism and hospitality industry (Jörling et al. 2019)

Augmented Reality and Virtual Reality

Advancement in AI has prompted the augmented reality (AR) and virtual reality (VR) technologies that have advanced rapidly as a prolific marketing technology to promote brands through use of headsets to stimulate shopping experience in consumer-to-consumer (C-to-C) BMs. Both AR and VR are increasingly becoming capable of enhancing customers' digital experiences and synchronizing digital touchpoints with traditional buying channels and conventional practices. Consumer dependence on AR and VR devices has significantly increased over time to capture virtual experience on home products, decor, appliances, and the like to contextualize virtual scenarios, for example, within a living room or a kitchen, to make appropriate decisions. Particularly in markets like travel, hospitality, and consumer retail, AR and VR have the potential to enhance customer experiences and reinforce their buying decision. Integrating AR and VR into e-commerce has significantly increased the firms' ability to provide customers with real, lifelike, and immersive preview of a product or brand. Both have further blended with industries to promote the B-to-B market segment, where consumers go for large and relatively sensitive shopping. In recent years, IKEA, LEGO, and physical fitness services like Peloton have experimented successfully with AR technology with headsets and mobile apps that allows customers to view the bottom line of their products and services and enable consumers to arrive at more appropriate purchase decision-making that aligns better with their needs.

The digital marketing strategies with hybrid self-experience stations attract more consumers to experience products online, develop and share their experience, and measure the perceived use value (satisfaction) of products. Such web exposure for products and services is accessible to many consumers today, which drives them to develop perceptions and attitude for products and services of their choice (Potter and Naidoo 2009). Both AI and collective intelligence enhance and complement each other and together serve as a hybrid concept. Both require training in personal development and high performance. The hybrid collective intelligence process coordinates with Industry 4.0 management processes and encourages firms and industries of various sizes to learn together. Many proximity-based ideas have benefited creative companies like LEGO, Samsung, and Sony (gaming division products) by reaching out to the crowd and specific user communities. The dynamic attributes of crowdsourcing of these companies have ranged from localization to globalization, disruption, and hybridization. However, while implementing society-linked BMs, companies tend to develop community hubs for customers and stakeholders to interact on face-to-face, digital, or hybrid communication models. The interactions of customers on these platforms help companies document the voice of customers to support strategy designs. Wisdom of crowd is a broad-spectrum cognitive pool, which contributes to collective intelligence with liberal thinking. Hybrid knowledge (a blend of conventional knowledge and technology-oriented knowledge) and group behavior have emerged as the principal source for firms to learn the perceptions of customers and stakeholders at large. The wisdom of the crowd is motivated by firms creating a free space for thinking together on a predetermined topic. The digital networks and the enhanced scope of interpersonal meetings among peers have helped collective intelligence grow manifold over the years. The brainstorming in the crowd-cognition process categorically exhibits individual and group behavior.

The real experience of products and services among consumers significantly helps industries where consumers make large and contextually sensitive purchases. In the real estate industry, several firms have experimented with AR and VR technologies that allow customers to view properties remotely and in a real ecological setup. Similarly, IKEA has started a successful AR mobile app that allows customers to view the furniture of IKEA in their own homes. VR devices add new experiences among consumers if designed properly. With this technology, customers can use their smartphones or webcams to remotely try on clothing, accessories, or makeup. AR and VR technologies have significantly transformed the fashion and beauty industries over the past with increasing confidence in sensory technologies among the firms and consumers.

AI-based robots, unlike machines with predefined functions, could revolutionize the retail industry by offering interactive solutions. Cutting-edge technologies significantly affect social and industrial development in transitional economies. The prominent technological edges that drive challenge-based research include AI, AR, VR, wearable technology, robotics, and Big Data analytics. The growing environmental concerns, public policies, and scientific communities describe the efforts that utilize ecosystem processes to boost challenge-based research in engineering and technology to address societal challenges. The challenge-based research outputs have significantly contributed to the development of the consumer sector economy (Rajagopal 2023).

The mainstream retailing industry has transformed from traditional shopping practices to multichannel retailing by developing retail businesses through e-commerce platforms. Such transformation in retailing technology has increased the global market outreach and online penetration of potential customers with increased visual satisfaction and ease-of-use of technology. The visualization features have allowed retailers to demonstrate the 3D store effect by allowing multiple presentations supported by visual technologies to provide sensory perceptions (Zha et al. 2022). Virtual merchandising blended with virtual store ergonomics, product dimensions, and sensory experience tends to instantly substitute the need for physical inspection such as fitness trials, touching, and appearance satisfaction. An effective merchandise display helps shoppers to coordinate a cross-product mix and develop purchase intentions. Visual merchandising stimulates self-image congruence, ontological reasoning, and neurobehavioral outcomes leading to perceptual stimuli and satisfaction reinforcing the feeling of seeing is experiencing. The positive attitude toward seeing, believing, and experiencing leads to a decision-making phenomenon within the perceptual triangle of elements comprising knowing, experiencing, and being. Virtual merchandising through clear arraying of product portfolios and simultaneous display of contextual products has given a wide range of options to consumers, which supports buying decisions and enables business model innovation among digital retail competitors (Mostaghel et al. 2022). One of the major impacts of digital technologies has been toward 3V factors—comprising Value Creation, Value Delivery, and Value Capture. Both AI and VR support consumer learning process in relation to product design, attributes, and values, which help consumers to make appropriate buying decisions quickly. In addition to AI and VR, chatbots and robot-driven responses have enhanced consumer experience online and supported consumer perceptions on seeing is experiencing.

The fusion of conventional communication, brick-and-mortar shopping behavior, and community interactions with technology-led virtual shopping experiences has provided consumers with a holistic experience of virtual merchandising and an integrated buying experience. Virtual communications supported by enhanced product information, real-time prices, customization advise, order and delivery tracking, and information on purchased transactions support consumer perceptions and purchase intentions on various retail technology platforms (Riegger et al. 2021). Fashion apparel is effectively promoted on social media mainly targeting Twitter (now X), Facebook, Instagram, and TikTok through emoticons, social speech tags, and unigrams and bigrams linguistic tags. Virtual display mannequins with anthropomorphic dimensions presenting human-like musculoskeletal morphology attract consumers to explore the array of products on virtual retail sites to make instant purchase decisions. In addition, embedded videos of models anchoring vogue products on virtual retailing websites stimulate appearance similarity, physical congruence, and social consciousness among consumers to inculcate purchase intentions (Song and Kim 2020).

The phenomenon of seeing-is-experiencing is founded on the maxims of visual perceptions, which leads to cognitive reasoning and developing perceptions on visual objects. Visual data are analyzed within internal neural space, form perceptual images, and drive cognitive reasoning through perceptual motions. Theories of visual perceptions argue that visual objects are perceived through neural networks and cognitive brain imaging to develop contextual semantics and decision-making by subjects. Visual perceptions are often sensitive to judgments, as inadequate construction of visual scenarios generates a gap between cognitive actualization and deception. Visual perceptions are affected by the quality of construction of visual scenario, cognitive inhibition, speed of visuals, and the combination of verbal (dynamic text) and nonverbal (contextual image, color, music, graphics, and appearance of anchors) elements. The scientific development on theory of visual perceptions has indicated several neural space dynamisms in mapping visual perceptions through visual pathways, optic tract, and topographical images (Jerath et al. 2018) within visual space. Visual perceptions are stimulated by motion and dynamics and oscillatory activities. These factors drive the brain activity for visual processing, decomposing information, and analyzing the effects of visual consciousness.

Voice Assistants in Shopping

The transcending marketing technology has been powered with AI-led platforms to assist consumers. Voice assistants are fundamentally AI-powered programs used by retail companies to help customers in preferential shopping, streamlining operations, and improving customer experience. Voice assistants are synchronized with voice-enabled technologies, such as smart speakers, to facilitate the shopping process and streamline interactions between consumers and virtual retailers. This approach enables users to search for products and place orders using various payment methods. Consumers are also able to track shipments and select to receive personalized suggestions using voice commands. They can also check prices and complete transactions without navigating through websites or apps. Voice assistants are able to create a more personalized shopping experience among consumers by analyzing previous purchases and preferences, track buying behavior, and suggest relevant products and offers. This can enhance customer satisfaction and increase the likelihood of repeat purchases and brand loyalty.

In addition, within a shopping mall, advertisements indicating maps and discount coupons are a form of localized proximity marketing.

Restaurants and fast-food outlets use mobile proximity marketing to show promotions to passers-by and attract them inside. They also show display advertisements about coupons to attract new customers and encourage existing customers to come back and experience repeat buying. Bluetooth beacon technology (BBT) enhances the scope of proximity marketing by fostering customers' reception of relationship marketing programs. By applying proximity BBT, firms can attain more accurate and detailed customer insights to better deliver the relationship programs to the right person at the right time and at the right location. Consequently, relationships with customers can be developed, maintained, and enhanced more efficiently and effectively than with the use of traditional proximity marketing technologies. Proximity BBT utilizes digital techniques to request permission to acquire data of customers via beacon systems to offer targeted relationship marketing tactics (Rajagopal 2023).

In addition to strengthening an inclusive shopping experience for consumers, who are not well acquainted with the Internet use and have difficulties in navigation over the website and would like to improve on traditional interfaces, voice search–assisted e-commerce provides a convenient and hands-free experience for online shoppers who might be multitasking. The intuitive nature of ordering by voice facilitates businesses selling grocery or home goods to consumer by creating good buying experience and value-driven satisfaction. Though most customer-centric businesses are increasingly developing voice search–friendly product descriptions and creating their own backend voice assistant products, the trend has been growing across both emerging markets and developed countries. For example, since 2017 Dominos has operated its own voice assistant embedded in their app for mobile devices through which customers can quickly order and track the preparation and delivery of a pizza ordered.

The chronological evolution of interactive marketing can be observed in the changing directions of the journey from broadcasting marketing (radio, catalogue, and physical mail) to electronic interactive marketing (television and telemarketing), and virtual marketing (seamless, smart television, smartphones, social media, and online marketing). The course of interactive marketing is changing continuously with the advancement of ICT. The global penetration of digital technologies and the diverse spread of social networks, blogs, and video platforms online have revolutionized the engagement of firms with consumers (Berezan et al. 2018). Interactive marketing today empowers consumers to raise voices both for and against the firm's innovation, manufacturing, distribution, and marketing policies. The interactive marketing on digital platforms has given an enormous rise to e-commerce supported by visual and functional technologies like AI, AR, and VR. Such advancements in technology have contributed to the conceptualization of metaverse as a virtual space for business. Some firms are also engaged in establishing connectivity between online and offline (O-to-O) to facilitate tangible shopping on metaverse (Rajagopal 2023).

Collective Intelligence

Crowdsourcing is a relatively new tool to have come into vogue that both regional and multinational companies increasingly use to generate ideas and communications and develop bottom-up BMs. Most multinational companies such as McDonald's, LEGO, Samsung, and Starbucks have successfully founded their growth on crowdsourced information. Such practice has changed the ways to analyze needs, attitudes, and behavior of consumer using collective intelligence tools and techniques. McDonald's invited ideas from customers to know their preferences on burgers. Upon analyzing the collective content, the company has been successful in marketing its products by ensuring customer value. The franchise exercised by customers in suggested competitive and local, value-based innovations in existing product lineup and toward development of new products catering to diverse customer's tastes had been a great contribution of crowd. Starbucks, an American coffee brewing company, has a strong presence in multiple social networks and regularly encourages consumers to submit, view, and discuss ideas along with employees from various Starbucks departments. The company has a dedicated website, which includes a leader board to track user-generated content. Similarly, LEGO, a creative toy company, allows users to design new products and simultaneously test the demand for new product. According to the company, any user can submit a design that other users are able to vote for. The idea with popular votes is accepted and moved to production. The creator receives a 1 percent royalty on the net revenue generated from utilizing the shared design idea (Rajagopal 2021).

The collective information repository serves as a source of open knowledge to the company and, at the same time, as a part of social movement to provide voice to customers to reach out to companies. This is an outside-in flow of information, which helps companies understand consumer perceptions, trends of referrals, and styles of customer advocacy on products and services. Nonetheless, collective intelligence has open information feeds that require companies to employ robust information filters for quality output. Most customer-centric companies have developed their social media page on Facebook to make customers stay abreast with information on new products and share their opinion on existing products and services. Some companies like Microsoft, Apple, and Amazon have also promoted customer communities wherein customers interact to share their experience and resolve problems. Discussions on companies' Facebook page and customer communities are periodically monitored and streamlined by designated employees and community leaders. Companies set the following crowdsourcing principles:

- Induct stimulant topics in business and society to attract crowd communication,
- Develop information screening processing and build information repositories to acquire and store information, and
- Analyze crowd communication systematically to use crowd input as the guide to business modeling and managing organizational performance.

Crowdsourced information enables companies to learn about customer perceptions and emotions through shared experience and values, cocreate products and services, and coevolve with customers against competitors. In addition, text mining has also emerged as a tool to do research on user-generated content across the web and derive necessary output on key terms. Text mining has become a popular qualitative research tool to extract meaningful data available in text form. Text-mining sources range from academic literature to online digital media such as social networking sites with user-generated content such as posts and comments about news, voice of the customer, speech-to-text data, and more tangible, digitally published documents (Jung and Lee 2020). Crowdsourcing practices are popular for cocreating product designs, problem-solving, and developing crowd-based BMs. The wisdom of crowds refers to the principle that the average view of a group of individuals on a given perspective can be similar or close to the acceptable response. It requires a large group of diverse opinions, but the collective error, the difference between the average opinion and the true value, remains small (Hertwig 2012).

Crowdsourcing or collective intelligence has emerged as a dynamic tool in the business ecosystem today, which is supported by stakeholders. It supports companies in cocreation and coevolution process with stakeholders through social interaction, social innovations, and social governance. Business ecosystems linked with sustainability goals drive public-private entrepreneurship (collaborations) to meet the United Nation's Sustainable Development Goals through social and frugal innovations. Crowd-based BMs emerge out of the collective intelligence generated through crowdsourcing. As crowdsourcing evolves, new research has identified a pitfall that companies should be alert to—consumer voting on ideas submitted on open innovation platforms is often skewed by social bias or people's tendency to like and vote for ideas whose progenitors have liked and voted for their own. Collective intelligence–led BMs rely more on consumer preference and social criteria while evaluating ideas generated through open innovation. Successful crowdsourcing ventures require more than an online platform and some kind of brand connection. Without an understanding of participant motivations and behaviors, casual attempts to leverage crowd wisdom may backfire and lead to unintended results. Prominent examples of crowdsourcing failures are myriad. Consider General Motors, which provided users with web tools to make their own ads for the Chevrolet Tahoe, resulting in a number of viral videos that lampooned the company's products and the American automotive industry's gas guzzlers more generally. In the fast-moving consumer goods industry, Mountain Dew successfully crowdsourced part of its product development through the Dewmocracy contest series, but a similar project asking fans to name the brand's new apple-flavored drink brought on a slew of ironic suggestions, including Diabeetus (Fedorenko et al. 2017).

Rapidly emerging new brands (with crowd-based ideas) from unfamiliar companies attract consumers with lower price offerings. Although most consumers tend to experiment with low-priced products and substitute for products that deliver satisfactory experience, they fail to develop sustainable perceptions and build an attitude toward repeat buying. However, industry attractiveness describes competition among traditional pipeline brands, which succeed by optimizing activities in their value chains. In addition, crowdsourcing and collective intelligence have helped companies and their brands to streamline themselves with customer perceptions, brand value, and competitiveness. Uber (transport service), Alibaba (e-commerce), and Airbnb (urban housing) are growing in the market by improving the consumer chain and delivering satisfaction through active customer engagement and collective intelligence (Van Alstyne et al. 2016).

Collective intelligence is also explorative, as it can connect firms with isolated business ideas with the success of such local experiments. The innovations developed in local markets are based on consumer needs and marketed within niche segments at an affordable price to consumers. These enterprises do not adapt to "design-to-market" innovation approach. However, innovations with utilitarian values tend to drive high demand in local markets as they match the sociocultural and ethnic values of their target market/audience. For example, in 2016, an engineer-entrepreneur of India designed a low-cost clay refrigerator, which requires no electricity and keeps the cooked food fresh and safe for 5 days uninterruptedly. This innovative product was branded as "*mittikool*" (clay-cool). It continued to function even in the event of irregular power supplies in rural areas. The concept of this innovation has been later adapted to the "design-to-market" strategy by a Chinese global giant Haier, which manufactured and commercialized non-compressor refrigerator. Instead of relying on a refrigerant, compressor, and evaporator to keep cool, it simply uses water and carbon dioxide (CO_2), plus a unique solid-state cooler. The product claims to save a significant amount of energy, provide more even cooling, eliminate all noise and vibration, and offer more usable space (Rajagopal 2020).

Case Studies

CS1: *Walmart Luminate and AI*

Walmart, a retail giant in the United States, is constantly working to improve customers' shopping experience through technology-led seamless omnichannel approach. This approach enables the firm to offer personalized experience to customers with valuable shopping insights. The radio frequency identification technology (RFID) has significantly improved the inventory management process through blockchain communication design. RFID technology has evoked a dynamic supply chain process, which offered unparalleled opportunity for collaboration with the firm. The firm has further stepped up its engagement with retailing technology and developed *Walmart Data Ventures' Walmart Luminate* by providing true omnichannel visibility to Walmart's merchants and suppliers. This data-driven approach has enormously motivated the managers to drive quicker and smarter business decisions and engage in sharper collaboration. The Walmart Data Ventures leadership and associates have collaborated with the Hershey Company to leverage Walmart Luminate to discover new opportunities studded by powerful data and analytics possibilities.

Walmart Data Ventures (2023) is a suite of data products that give U.S.-based merchants and suppliers an unprecedented access to rich, aggregated, customer insights that enable managers in data-driven macro- and micro-level decision-making. Within the closed-loop data system, Walmart Luminate uses advanced data science tools and techniques to collect consumer and market data from across the omnichannel path. The synthesis helps the firm's managers and collaborators to analyze shopper behavior and channel performance, gather input directly from customers, test new growth strategies, and measure the impact. Walmart Luminate includes three modules, which address shopper behavior, channel performance, and customer perception to improve collaboration of merchants and suppliers. It has emerged as an easier omni-view option to measure customer habits and needs in a dynamic, user-friendly digital shopping environment.

Walmart has integrated generative artificial intelligence (AI) across its business operations using the transformative technology to drive performance and deliver better service to customers. Walmart has been successful in piloting the generative AI chatbot to measure customer preferences and sales trends of specific brands and close deals with suppliers of slow-moving items. Of those suppliers, the chatbot helped with closing 64 percent bad deals, gaining an average of 1.5 percent in cost-savings and helped to settle with an extended payment possibility. Walmart has come forward with the AI-supported technology to induct robots in some of its stores and warehouses to manage inventory, order processing, and online-to-offline (O-to-O) order processing and delivering tasks. Walmart uses AI-powered robots to retrieve products from online orders and deliver them to in-store workstations. Walmart also uses small robots in some stores to pick and pack online grocery orders. Walmart previously used robots from Bossa Nova Robotics to scan shelves and ensure items were in stock and prices were accurate. However, its partnership terminated with Bossa Nova in 2020 after deciding that people could do the same work. Walmart uses robots and scanners in its warehouses to track goods as they arrive and are stored (Albrecht 2020). Nonetheless, Walmart aims to get 65 percent of its stores in the United States fully automated by 2026. The company is investing heavily in technology to improve its supply chain to sustain its "Every Day Low Prices" mission.

The retailing technology at Walmart has been further advanced with the use of Voice Order service, which allows customers to connect the Walmart voice order app on their mobile devices and home smart speakers to their Walmart account and order products by speaking out loud. In addition, there is also a Text-to-Shop feature that lets customers ask for what they want by texting Walmart. With a simple AI-powered text-chat technology, customers can search for items, add or remove products from their cart, reorder products, and schedule a delivery or pickup. The online AI shopping assistant of the firm is designed to help shoppers find the best products for their needs or even plan the perfect event with the generative AI voice assistants. Walmart has introduced a conversational AI called Ask Sam for in-store associates. The firm saw the use of AI-based retailing technology enabled it to reduce millions of customer contacts by immediately providing answers to questions about returns, order status, and more. This real-time conversational functionality of Walmart is available across multiple countries, including the United States, Canada, Mexico, and Chile (Marr 2024).

CS2: Technology in ALDO Canadian Shoe Company

ALDO Shoes was founded in Canada in 1972. The company originated with footwear stores in Montreal, Ottawa, Quebec City, and Winnipeg. Aldo Bensadoun, the founder of this company, is recognized today as a global shoe giant from Canada. In its early days, the company's footwear suppliers were located in Italy, and the company established direct terms for trade with the Italian manufacturers by eliminating the middlemen between Canada and European manufacturers. The brand expanded in the 1980s and 1990s, with stores operating under the name Aldo across Canada. The first store outside of North America opened in Israel in 1995. The brand expanded in the 2000s—it set up outlets in Saudi Arabia, in 2001; England, in 2002; and Singapore, in 2003. Since then, the ALDO Group, with the Aldo and Spring banners, has further expanded on the international market.

The company launched the *Transit* banner in Canada, which later became *Spring* upon its launch in the United States. Five years later, the brand was enriched with *Feetfirst* banner, which caters to an older clientele. Additionally, the company operates *Globo Shoes* to address the family market. In 2010, the company once again began to evolve when it introduced, in Canada, a new store concept called *Locale* that replaced the current Feetfirst stores. Locale is a footwear and accessories boutique-style concept store aimed at young professionals, which offers a number of brand names. Since 2015, e-commerce was transforming the face of retailing, and ALDO with a global presence had to digitize its marketing and sales operations to enter into the e-commerce segment by adapting the gearing-up retaining technology. The effects of e-commerce were felt not just in the sales channels but also in the firm's digital endeavors to generate total customer experience through a technology-driven customer journey. To successfully execute a compelling online and overseas strategy, there were a few approaches that ALDO needed to revise, which included its franchising model, international business model, and omnichannel marketing strategy (Toulan and Huang 2018). However, ALDO has restructured its business model under the Companies' Creditors Arrangement Act citing the impact of the COVID-19 pandemic. As many as 6,680 store associates had to shut down, and more than half of the employees at its headquarters were laid off.

Overcoming the constraints of the pandemic, ALDO has developed a machine-learning model, *Delphine,* to avoid overstocking or understocking while optimizing its inventory management processes. This model focuses on more creative tasks, such as fashion trend predictions, while providing them with an analytical starting point for demand forecasting. ALDO Group leveraged a Canadian government subsidy to develop Delphine, a predictive machine-learning model that helped the company manage just-in-time inventory across its supply chain channels and ensure distribution from in-store to TikTok Shop. Additionally, ALDO Group is helping to develop a generative AI model that aims to provide shoppers with customized product recommendations based on particular celebrities and online influencers. Predictive AI and machine learning have been instrumental in transforming ALDO's approach to innovation. Associating generative AI proved useful for the company in developing trendy design footwear, promoting premier brands and organizing the fashion runway shows twice a year with AI-led applications.

ALDO Group is engaged in developing a generative AI model that lets shoppers receive personalized product recommendations based on a particular celebrity. For example, a shopper can request—"I need to look like a specific celebrity," and the model will generate an image with recommend shoes in a conversational way. In Delphine, it was determined that the model could add marginal gross profit at the experimental stage and may contribute in the 5 years of its adoption with an increase in profit margin between 5 and 7 percent. The company held its first Retail Gen AI Hackathon in collaboration with McGill University in Montreal and Amazon Web Services. It led to a plan to revamp ALDO's online product search functions and enhance product recommendations. Generative AI is still in seeding stages, but it can help generate text, help in search engine optimization, and offer product descriptions, while predictive AI model can help forecast demand and sales and plan for discount optimization.

Summary

The rapid advances in information and communication technology (ICT) have significantly impacted the digital revolution in business and have encouraged firms to adapt to automation technologies to improve their manufacturing, logistics, and marketing operations. Gen AI has taken all industries by storm, and retail is one of the leading sectors where the application of advanced AI applications can bring many benefits. Areas where retail executives are looking to deploy AI include personalization, supply chain management, and security. The integration of digital information with augmented reality (AR) technology helps synchronize the digital realm with physical environment to offer users a real-time, in-person shopping experience. In a physical store, consumers are motivated by sensory stimuli provided by AR, which, in turn, reinforces their desire to shop. The integration of AI with advanced AR and VR tools and the Metaverse allows for immersive shopping experiences, with AI curating personalized product showrooms and virtual assistants to guide users. AI has demonstrated its successful contribution to the dynamic pricing used by airlines in passenger ticketing, Uber services, and pricing of accommodation in the hospitality industry, including in particular Airbnb services. AI in marketing has a new space to grow in customer-centric firms. AI has gone beyond robotics structures for customers, as it is now emerging as a tool for decision-making in consumer-oriented firms.

The recent technology development has introduced generative AI in marketing operations among firms engaged in the B-to-C, B-to-B, hybrid, and D-to-C segments and has opened up greater opportunities for value-creating personalization among consumers, using dynamic pricing, developing user-friendly chatbots, creating voice- and virtual assistants, and improving the customer search to enhance the proximity of market to both existing and new geodemographic consumer segments. Broadly, the marketing technology includes integration of AI and machine learning. In addition, AR, VR, and MXR along with the Internet of Things (IoT) combine several Internet-based devices to enable monitoring and control. VR creates immersive, computer-generated environments that simulate real or fantasy objects within a chosen or predetermined ambience while the IoT is the next milestone in technological growth that has significantly affected product market, industry, and quality and lifestyle of users as it connects physical devices to the Internet allowing them to collect and exchange data to help monitor and control various processes and transactions. Another stage of technological growth along with extensive applications of AI is machine learning, which largely supports data-based decisions in business and industry. Machine learning relies heavily on data. Voice assistants are synchronized with voice-enabled technologies, such as smart speakers, to facilitate the shopping process and streamline interactions between consumers and virtual retailers. This approach enables users to search for products and place orders using various payment methods.

Crowdsourcing and collective intelligence have emerged as dynamic tools in the business ecosystem today, which is supported by stakeholders. They support companies to engage in cocreation and coevolution process with stakeholders through social interaction, social innovations, and social governance. Collective intelligence is also explorative, as it is able to connect firms with isolated business ideas with success of such local experiments. The innovations developed in local markets are based on consumer needs and marketed within niche segments at an affordable price to consumers. These enterprises do not adapt to "design-to-market" innovation approach.

References

Albrecht, C. 2020. *Walmart to Stop Using Bossa Nova's Shelf-Scanning Robots*. The Spoon, November 2. https://thespoon.tech/report-walmart-to-stop-using-bossa-novas-shelf-scanning-robots/.

Avery, J., A. Israeli, and E. von Maur. 2021. *THE YES: Reimagining the Future of e-Commerce with Artificial Intelligence*. Cambridge, MA: Harvard Business School Publishing.

Berezan, O., A. S. Krishen, S. Agarwal, and P. Kachroo. 2018. "The Pursuit of Virtual Happiness: Exploring the Social Media Experience Across Generations." *Journal of Business Research* 89: 455–61.

Boghin, J. 2014. *Three Ways Companies Can Make Co-Creation Payoff*. McKinsey & Company.

Buhalis, D., T. Harwood, V. Bogicevic, G. Viglia, S. Beldona, and C. Hofacker. 2019. "Technological Disruptions in Services: Lessons from Tourism and Hospitality." *Journal of Service Management* 30 (4): 484–506.

Fedorenko, I., P. Berthon, and T. Rabinovich. 2017. "Crowded Identity: Managing Crowdsourcing Initiatives to Maximize Value for Participants Through Identity Creation." *Business Horizons* 60 (2): 155–65.

GrandViewResearch. 2024. "Marketing Technology, Market Size, and Trends." *Market Analysis Report.* Accessed November 14, 2024. https://www.grandviewresearch.com/industry-analysis/marketing-technology-martech-market-report.

Grewal, D., A. L. Roggeveen, and J. Nordfält. 2017. "The Future of Retailing." *Journal of Retailing* 93 (1): 1–6.

Haenlein, M., and A. Kaplan. 2019. "A Brief History of Artificial Intelligence: On the Past, Present, and Future of Artificial Intelligence." *California Management Review* 61 (4): 5–14.

Hertwig, R. 2012. "Tapping into the Wisdom of the Crowd-With Confidence." *Science* 336: 303–4.

Holman, J., and K. Huang. 2023. "The Companies Trying to Make Live Shopping a Thing in the U.S." *New York Times*, May 10.

Jerath, R., S. M. Cearley, V. A. Barnes, and M. Jensen. 2018. "Micro-Calibration of Space and Motion by Photoreceptors Synchronized in Parallel with Cortical Oscillations: A Unified Theory of Visual Perception." *Medical Hypotheses* 110: 71–5.

Jörling, M., R. Böhm, and S. Paluch. 2019. "Service Robots: Drivers Perceived Responsibility for Service Outcomes." *Journal of Service Research* 22 (4): 404–20.

Jung, H., and B. G. Lee. 2020. "Research Trends in Text Mining: Semantic Network and Main Path Analysis of Selected Journals. *Expert Systems with Applications* 162 (in press). https://doi.org/10.1016/j.eswa.2020.113851.

Lamberton, C., and A. T. Stephen. 2016. "A Thematic Exploration of Digital, Social Media, and Mobile Marketing: Research Evolution from 2000 to 2015 and an Agenda for Future Inquiry." *Journal of Marketing* 80 (6): 146–72.

Leung, C. H., and W. T. Yan-Chan. 2020. "Retail Chatbots: The Challenges and Opportunities of Conversational Commerce." *Journal of Digital & Social Media Marketing* 8 (1): 68–84.

Marr, B. 2024. "The Amazing Ways Walmart Is Using Generative AI." *Forbes*, February 15. https://www.forbes.com/sites/bernardmarr/2024/02/15/the-amazing-ways-walmart-is-using-generative-ai/.

Mostaghel, R., P. Oghazi, V. Parida, and V. Sohrabpour. 2022. "Digitalization Driven Retail Business Model Innovation: Evaluation of Past and Avenues for Future Research Trends." *Journal of Business Research* 146: 134–45.

Potter, C., and G. Naidoo. 2009. "Evaluating Large-scale Interactive Radio Programs. *Distance Education* 30 (1), 117–41.

Rajagopal. 2020. *Transgenerational Marketing: Evolution, Expansion, and Experience.* Palgrave Macmillan.

Rajagopal. 2021. *Crowd-Based Business Models—Using Collective Intelligence for Market Competitiveness.* Cham, Switzerland: Springer.

Rajagopal. 2022. "Impact of Retail Technology During Business Shutdown." *Marketing Intelligence and Planning* 40 (4): 441–59.

Rajagopal. 2023. *Proximity Marketing: Converging Community, Consciousness, and Consumption.* New York: Business Expert Press.

Renko, S., and M. Druzijanic. 2014 "Perceived Usefulness of Innovative Technology in Retailing: Consumers' and Retailers' Point of View." *Journal of Retailing and Consumer Services,* 21 (5), 836–43.

Riegger, A. S., J. F. Klein, K. Merfeld, and S. Henkel. 2021. "Technology-Enabled Personalization in Retail Stores: Understanding Drivers and Barriers." *Journal of Business Research* 123: 140–55.

Song, S. Y., and Y. K. Kim. 2020. "Factors Influencing Consumers' Intention to Adopt Fashion Robot Advisors: Psychological Network Analysis." *Clothing and Textiles Research Journal* 40 (1): 3–18.

Statista. (n.d.). "eCommerce—Worldwide." Accessed November 10, 2024. https://www.statista.com/outlook/emo/ecommerce/worldwide?currency=usd.

Toulan, O., and S. H. Huang. 2018. *ALDO's Global Omnichannel Imperative.* Cambridge, MA: Harvard Business School Publishing.

Van Alstyne, M. W., G. Parker, and S. P. Choudary. 2016. "Pipelines, Platforms, and the New Rules of Strategy." *Harvard Business Review* 94 (4): 54–62.

Walmart Data Ventures. 2023. "Insights from Walmart Luminate Make Innovation and Collaboration Sweeter." Accessed November 12, 2024. https://p2pi.com/walmart-luminate-goes-international.

Zha, D., P. Foroudi, T. C. Melewar, and Z. Jin. 2022. "Experiencing the Sense of the Brand: The Mining, Processing and Application of Brand Data Through Sensory Brand Experiences." *Qualitative Market Research* 25 (2): 205–32.

CHAPTER 2

Virtual Business Modeling

Overview

Advancement of technology-led business modeling is founded on the cyber–physical marketing trends, ease-of-use of technology, and perceived use value of consumers in adapting to changing online shopping technologies. This chapter focuses on the strategic (long-term) virtual business modeling using advanced e-commerce designs and radical marketing-mix comprising 27 elements overshadowing the conventional 4Ps of Product, Price, Place, and Promotions. In addition, the chapter discusses the business canvas–marketing modeling fit to improve the performance of virtual marketing. Other topics discussed here include emerging trends on VSC management and their integration with the virtual business modeling. One major challenge for e-commerce in connecting people to business is the cyber–physical engagement of consumers and behavioral proximity emphasizing the role of interactive marketing on cyber space with the support of ICT, which constitutes the core discussion in this chapter.

E-commerce Business Models

Virtual business modeling is different from the brick-and-mortar retailing business model, as it has high agility that can be extended to various customer segments by integrating both forward and reverse logistics and online payment options, unlike retailing in physical stores. Market trends and consumer behavior are rapidly changing, and social media is playing a critical role in determining marketing decisions. Volatility of consumer markets can have significant negative effects on market share, profitability, and brand equity of companies. However, volatility is an embedded attribute of competitive growth theory. The argument central to the theory of change management is that companies operating in a competitive business environment consider consumer preferences, innovation, technology, and growth-related investments as dynamic variables. The interplay of consumers within the social (interpersonal) and digital (remote response) platforms also helps companies to adapt to inclusive BMs and stay distinctive in the competitive marketplace. Consumers today are increasingly looking for brands that have a social purpose that goes beyond functional and competitive benefits associated with a product or service or brand. As a result, most companies are taking social stand in highly visible ways. An effective, convergent business strategy creates social and customer values by coevolving the brand in the e-commerce business model (Rajagopal 2024).

E-commerce has evolved with the concept of consumer product marketing with a focus on serving the B-to-C market segment. Virtual businesses targeting the B-to-C segment are engaged in selling consumer products directly to end-users. The decision-making process for online purchase is very agile, and the purchase information can be stored in the customer account with the e-commerce company. Firms following the B-to-C model sell products directly to consumers through their own websites or physical stores like Amazon and local boutiques. The online e-commerce platforms connect buyers and sellers through the third-party suppliers or from their inventory of pre-procured products, similar to the practice of Amazon. The third-party supplier-based marketing firms like Expedia (travel and hospitality services) and Etsy (ethnic products e-commerce) also fall into the B-to-C business segment. Online customer-centric e-commerce companies largely attract consumers through extensive advertisements on the Internet by analyzing the consumer search behavior data provided by AI. The B-to-C e-commerce platforms build online communities around shared interests and target their ads to these groups. Social media sites like Facebook and Instagram are prime examples of community-based B-to-C e-commerce platforms. However, some businesses charge a subscription fee for access to their content or services. Streaming services like Netflix operate on this model.

E-commerce has another growing segment—industrial marketing, also known as B-to-B marketing—which involves marketing of goods and services from one business to another. Unlike consumer marketing that targets individual consumers, industrial marketing focuses on businesses, manufacturers, and other organizations. The sales process in industrial marketing is often more complex and involves multiple stages, such as requests for proposals, tenders, and contract negotiations to arrive at executable terms of reference. E-commerce oriented toward B-to-B requires businesses to develop strategic relationships with clients and maintain a tactical edge in negotiation to gain competitive advantage in the boundary-less marketplace. These relationships are often based on trust and reliability. Industrial clients demand customized solutions of products and services, which needs a deeper understanding of client's business and industry. Accordingly, purchases are typically made by professional buyers based on the derived demand; their expert opinions on the product and services to be delivered carry weight and influence purchase decisions.

Udaan is a growing B-to-B e-commerce firm based in India, connecting manufacturers, wholesalers, and retailers across various categories of products like FMCG, electronics, staples, fruits and vegetables, allowing small and medium businesses to buy products online at competitive prices through a digital marketplace. *Udaan* began operations in 2016 as a middle-ground entity to streamline multi-brand wholesale and retail operations, eliminating middlemen in B-to-B transactions. *Udaan* targeted small and medium enterprises. The earlier product distribution chain in B-to-B was long, inefficient, and highly disjointed. The emergence of m-commerce, deepening the penetration of smartphones in the region and the government's increased interest in digitization, leveraged the B-to-B e-commerce space. While most players adopted a vertically based business model focused on specific product categories, *Udaan* pursued top-line growth and attacked the sector's inefficiencies with a horizontal, cross-category business model.

In addition to the B-to-C and B-to-B e-commerce BMs, consumer-to-consumer (C-to-C) e-commerce is an emerging business model where consumers sell goods or services directly to other consumers within the community typically through an online platform or through social media channels. Popular C-to-C platforms include eBay, Etsy, Craigslist, and Facebook Marketplace, which facilitate transactions by providing a space for consumers to list items for sale and for buyers to find what they need. The rise of m-commerce engaging customers through mobile apps and social media channels has significantly boosted the popularity of C-to-C e-commerce, making it easier for consumers to buy and sell items without territorial boundaries. Quality control and payment security can be issues, as transactions are between individuals rather than through a business. Platforms often implement policies to mitigate these risks. The prominent C-to-C e-commerce company Etsy was launched in 2005 and has gone public with successful IPO (initial public offer) execution. The Etsy business model is based on a multisided e-commerce platform focused on handcrafted goods. Etsy charges sellers at least $0.20 for each product they list on the platform, and the listing is valid for 4 months. If there are multiple quantities of the same item, the listing fee will be automatically renewed after the sale of each of the items listed. This is a revenue stream for the company, as lots of products are listed regularly on Etsy. Sellers must pay required commission to the firms (3.5 percent) on the amount of each sale performed on the platform. Sellers can advertise their items or shops on the platform (The Business Model Analyst 2023). The ads are charged on a cost-per-click (CPC) basis. Sellers can also build a personalized website to sell their products inside the platform by paying a prescribed fee.

Similar to the B-to-C business model of e-commerce, the direct-to-consumer (D-to-C) marketing is also a significantly growing business model through which firms sell their products or services directly to consumers, without involving middlemen like retailers, vendors, or third-party sellers (3PS). Brands following this model have more control over their marketing operations, customer relationships, and customer experience. Selling the DTC brands to customers incurs lower costs than brick-and-mortar retailing due to fewer business components like employees, purchasing costs, and mailing confirmation. Personalization is a powerful tool for DTC business. Firms engaged in DTC marketing process extensively use information on customers' interests, purchase history, and browsing behavior to craft targeted virtual campaigns through e-mails and SMS for each individual customer. Social media marketing is also embedded in DTC marketing strategy. The influencer marketing reinforces the DTC marketing approach on social media channels. The DTC marketing approach largely involves subscription-based customer deals that help firms to acquire and retain customers. *Barkbox*, a DTC startup founded in 2011, offers a monthly subscription to a box of oral hygiene products, curated treats, toys, and other essentials for pets like dogs and cats. The startup has shipped more than 10 million boxes. *Barkbox* and North Star Acquisition Corporation merged in 2020, and the value of *Barkbox* post-merger stood at approximately US$1.6 billion. The BARK has become a publicly listed company on the New York Stock Exchange.

Another business model that emerged during the COVID-19 pandemic was converging the online ordering and offline delivery as a hybrid strategy with less waiting time and touch-less delivery of orders. This approach has become a part of retailers' e-commerce practice irrespective of their size and market share. The click-and-collect or online-to-offline marketing, often abbreviated as O-to-O, refers to a marketing strategy where businesses use online channels like websites and social media to attract customers to make purchases in their physical stores, essentially bridging the gap between digital and physical shopping experiences. O-to-O business model aims to drive traffic from online engagement to offline sales at a brick-and-mortar location. One of the underlying objectives in this business strategy is to create a smooth transition for customers between online browsing and in-store purchases. Consumers get more time for online product selection by doing market research prior to deciding about buying a product, with the level of proximity and convenience in relation to the distance between the in-store pickup location and the point of order delivery playing a key role in purchase decision. The O-to-O business model allows hybrid retailers to enhance the outreach of online platforms while capitalizing on the benefits of physical store interaction, like product testing and immediate gratification.

E-commerce Ecosystem

The core and contextual attributes form the ecosystem of a business, which is a strategic perspective of managing business in a competitive marketplace. The notion of business ecosystem addresses the relative concepts of collaboration and competition, such as customer-centric and market-led strategies of business in both predetermined and dynamic business systems. Broadly, the extrinsic attributes of a business ecosystem include innovation (social and market-based), a competition constituent (opportunity mapping, elements of oligopoly and monopsony, and market taxonomy), and social business philosophies of companies (Parente et al. 2018). Traditional firms considered macro elements of business as exogenous drivers of the business ecosystem and focused on controllable variables like organizational design, work culture, and marketing-mix. Exogenous elements like competitors, suppliers, stakeholders, and business partners have become endogenous management factors of the business ecosystem. Technology plays a major role in the business ecosystem today, which has evolved from an internally focused attribute to customer-facing attributes, leading to agile business development. The bilateral factors in the business ecosystem include government, business partners (manufacturing, logistics, and marketing), financial institutions, and information technology providers. The contemporary marketing philosophy is founded on a polyhedron framework that has a triangular prismatic effect with five faces, six edges, and nine vertices. The philosophical thoughts on modern business can be stretched wide from the geometric structure to the functional propositions in the marketplace, which entails broadly the market, society, and customer values. The variables embedding the faces, edges, and vertices of the prismatic structure of marketing are exhibited in Figure 2.1.

The prismatic structure of marketing management has five faces (F1–F5), six vertices (V1–V6), and nine edges (E1–E9) that help managers to develop marketing strategies, processes, and make competitive decisions as exhibited Figure 2.1. The faces of marketing prism constitute manufacturers spread across the global, local, and niche destinations supported by suppliers and logistics operators constituting supply chain on regular, contractual, and casual terms of reference, including the third-party suppliers (3PS) who provide both forward and reverse logistics in the e-commerce process. Other faces of the prismatic e-commerce structure include retailers of different sizes (mega, large, medium, and small), direct and indirect service providers, and consumers across the geodemographic segments. There are six vertices of the e-commerce prism encompassing innovation (basic, trendy, and luxury products), technology (concerns on cost-time-risk), industry attractiveness (new entrants, substitution effects, bargaining with suppliers and customers, and rivalry in industry), business segments, proximity to society, and cyber-regulations. The operational span of business segments constitutes another vertex of the prismatic structure of e-commerce, which serves B-to-C, B-to-B, C-to-C,

Prismatic Edges (E1-E9)
- Organizational culture
- Collective intelligence
- Artificial intelligence
- Data analytics
- Business canvas
- Interactive platforms
- Social commerce
- Customer value creation

Prismatic Vertices (V1-V6)
- Innovation (basic needs and luxury)
- Technology (cost-time-risk)
- Industry attractiveness
- Business segments
  - B2C, B2B, C2C, D2C, O2O
- Society, culture, and proximity
- Cyber regulations

- Market leadership and competitiveness
- Customer acquisition and retention
- Marketing strategies and tactics

3-D Prismatic Structure of E-commerce

Prismatic Faces (F1–F5)
- Manufacturers
- Suppliers
- Retail departments
- Service providers (logistics)
- Consumers

V_3, E_6, V_4, F_2, E_8, E_7, E_5, V_6, $F_{4\ Back}$, $F_{5\ Base}$, E_9, $F_{3\ Front}$, E_4, V_2, E_2, F_1, V_5, E_3, E_1, V_1

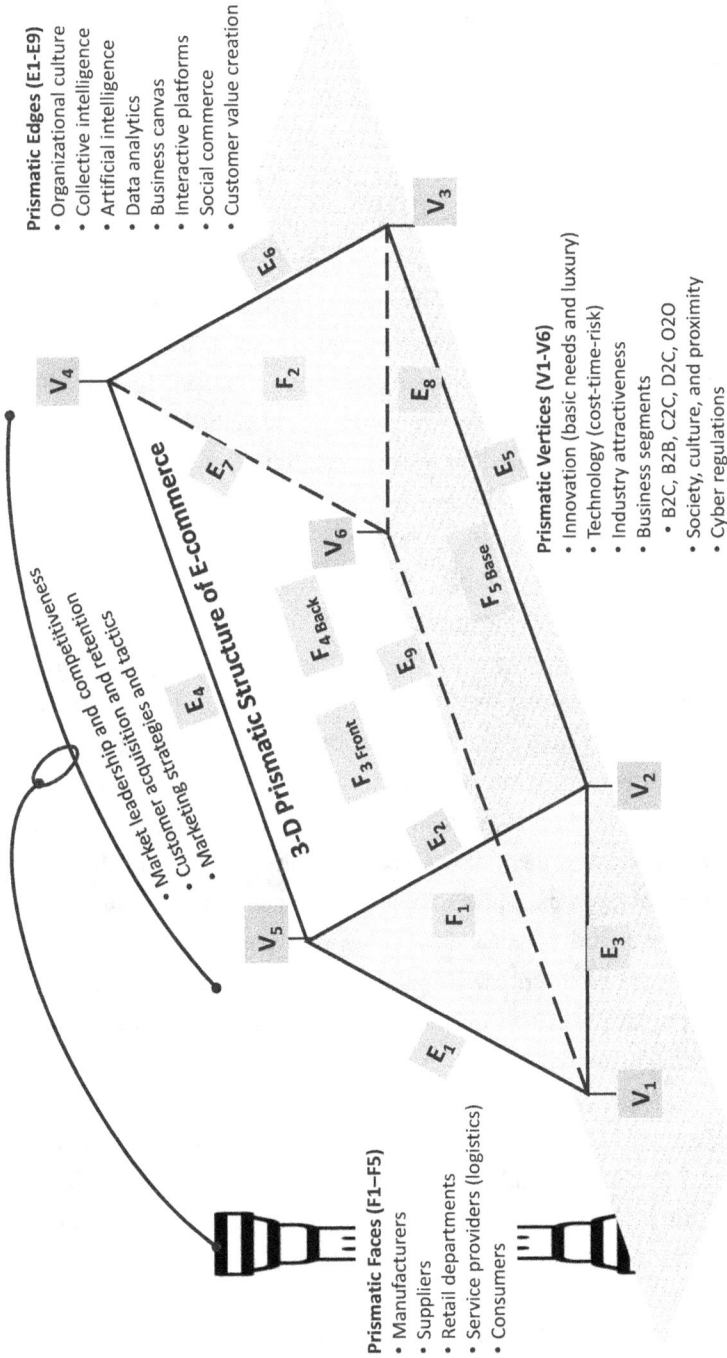

Figure 2.1 Prismatic representation of e-commerce elements

DTC, and O-to-O consumer segments. Extensive operations in various consumer segments increase the proximity of e-commerce operations across different social and cultural settings (V5). The cyber-regulations to protect data breach and streamline ethical business operations online form the last vertex (V6) of the e-commerce prismatic structure.

The elements of vertices of prismatic e-commerce structure as discussed above help managers to define governance, openness, action, and learning continuum (GOAL) necessary for business growth in the competitive environment. Innovations supported by crowd impetus through collective intelligence, cocreation, and coevolution help firms in seeding new product ideas in the utilitarian and hedonic market segments. Rapidly growing technologies are often attractive to embed innovations, but they need to be scrutinized for relative cost, time, risk, and derived value propositions. Consequently, these edges of marketing prism are sensitive to the PNS (problems, needs, and solutions) factors to explore consumer problems, assess needs, and offer appropriate solutions within the industry and market ecosystems. Innovation, technology, and collective intelligence drive industry to a competitive dome, and induce internal rivalry and competition among the firms to exploit existing opportunities and stay ahead of the leadership race. Nonetheless, society and government also play a significant role in marketing management, and good office management practices recommend firms to develop proximity with society and the government. The social proximity of the firm helps in developing social consciousness among its consumers on corporate policies, ethics, values, and sustainability. Though government interventions in marketing are often criticized, public policies on pricing, distribution, advertising, and social media engagements are necessary to be brought under categorical public policies to protect the interest of stakeholders and consumers.

There are nine edges in managing virtual commerce as illustrated in Figure 2.1, which include organizational culture and behavior of marketing firms, relationship management, interactive marketing, business canvas, marketing-mix, sustainability, leadership, empowerment, and customer outreach. The vertices support any straight or angular structure in a construction with defined design. Likewise, the above vertices streamline decision-making, strategy development, and value creation processes in marketing despite changing market dynamics and disruptive influences. Organizational culture and behavior of a marketing firm need to integrate panoramic attributes of consumers, suppliers, manufacturers, and competitors. In a broad contemporary perspective, competition in the marketplace today can be managed through different modes of cooperation, such as strategic alliances. Managing relationship with key partners and consumers is another important vertex in the prismatic marketing model that encourages relationship marketing to enhance satisfaction, value co-creation and promote social business perspective of firms in all segments of businesses, including in B-to-B, B-to-C, C-to-C, and O-to-O business segments. The relationship marketing is further strengthened by interactions between firms' key partners, stakeholders, and consumers on social media channels. Such interactions may be both longitudinal (with specific clients over long time) and latitudinal (across geodemographic segments). Besides the socialization of business through developing relationships and interactive transversalities across the consumer population, firms seek to strengthen their business foundations by building business canvas[2] and marketing-mix[3] block by block to gain market leadership. Empowering consumers and engaging them emotionally with the company in marketing activities help firms in narrowing their social proximity, generating social consciousness, and leveraging the geographic and ethnic outreach of consumers.

Collective intelligence emerging from analyzing crowd behavior through qualitative and quantitative data helps e-commerce firms understand consumer preferences and their willingness to pay for products and inculcate perceived value propositions. Artificial intelligence (AI) has been instrumental in designing interactive platforms to boost social commerce and value creation, besides improving the operational efficiency of firms engaged in virtual business. One of the principal elements of the vertices of prismatic business structure of e-commerce is the integration

---

[2]Business Canvas has universal nine elements consisting of key partners, key resources, key activities, customer relationship, segmentation, distribution channels, value proposition, cost structure, and revenue stream.

[3]The advanced marketing-mix has eleven core elements known as 11Ps comprising product, price, place, promotion, packaging, pace, people, promotion, psychodynamics, posture, and proliferation (Rajagopal, 2019)

of business canvas with nine elements to improve competitiveness in business: key objectives, key resources, key partners, customer relations, segmentation, value proposition, channel management, cost structure, and revenue stream.

Advanced Marketing-Mix

Microeconomic factors have a key presence in a company's business environment, and they guide the company in managing its competitiveness in the destination market. The microeconomic factors, on the other hand, are largely woven around the marketing-mix followed by the company. Globalization has largely altered the conventional marketing-mix, and now there 11 key elements of marketing-mix referred to as the 11Ps of business, including the conventional 4Ps of Product, Price, Place, and Promotion. The additional 7Ps added to the original 4Ps are summed up as follows: 5Ps including Packaging, Pace (competitive dynamics), People (front-liners in marketing), Performance, and Psychodynamics (peer-to-peer, word-of-mouth, or the grapevine effect) constitute the extended operational factors of marketing-mix; there are two more Ps known as corporate factors, namely, Posture (corporate image) and Proliferation (product and market diversification). This new marketing-mix concept has become an essential part of marketing practices of multinational companies. The integration of 11Ps in a marketing-mix strategy is both effective and simple. Interconnecting the marketing-mix elements such as product, price, packaging, and promotion with psychodynamics and posture, companies may gain sustainable competitive advantage, like Samsung in the consumer electronics product markets, and Walmart in global retailing sector. By applying marketing-mix, companies can attain consistency, integration, and leverage in a marketing program to fit the needs of marketplace (Rajagopal 2011). Customer-centric companies in oligopolistic market can protect their stakeholder value, increase market share, reduce incidences of customer defection, and minimize the probability of market fragmentation by adapting to the following strategy in their marketing-mix:

- Product (attributes mapping, complementarity of products, and product lifecycle)

- Price (competitive pricing)
- Place (360° availability, convenience, faster and secured deliveries)
- Promotion (hands-on and future benefits and value additions)
- Packaging (attractive, stackable, and cost-effective)
- Pace (first-mover advantage)
- People (high standards of customer relations, responsiveness, and sensitive to clients)
- Performance (cocreating consumer surplus, reinforcing values, and lessons drawn from product-line performance)
- Psychodynamics (creating consumer communities, encouraging digital interface, experience-sharing, triggering grapevine effect, crowdsourcing ideas, and managing diffusion of values)
- Posture (reinforcing corporate image, encouraging consumer engagement, codesigning products and strategies, developing differentiated niches to cater to consumer values by geodemographic attributes)
- Proliferation (customer-centric product diversification, introducing servitization policies, planning value-based market expansion, and developing competitive differentiation).

The advanced marketing-mix has two layers to support the decision-making and develop competitive marketing strategies. These layers can be identified as core and peripheral levels, which include the 11Ps listed above and a variety of supporting elements comprising 4As, 4Cs, 4Vs, and 4Es. In all, the advanced marketing-mix consists of 27 elements that influence managerial decision-making. The advanced marketing-mix and their attributes are exhibited in Figure 2.2.

The foundation and business structure of e-commerce is based on the core and advanced marketing-mix to enhance proximity, processes of procurement, packaging, order management, delivery of order, reverse logistics, and analyzing customer feedback as illustrated in Figure 2.2. The core and peripheral marketing-mix elements are discussed in detail in the following section. However, it is necessary for managers to learn about several factors at the macro- and micro-market levels, which significantly affect strategy development aimed at gaining competitive advantage and enhancing the market share. Such factors include consumer behavior,

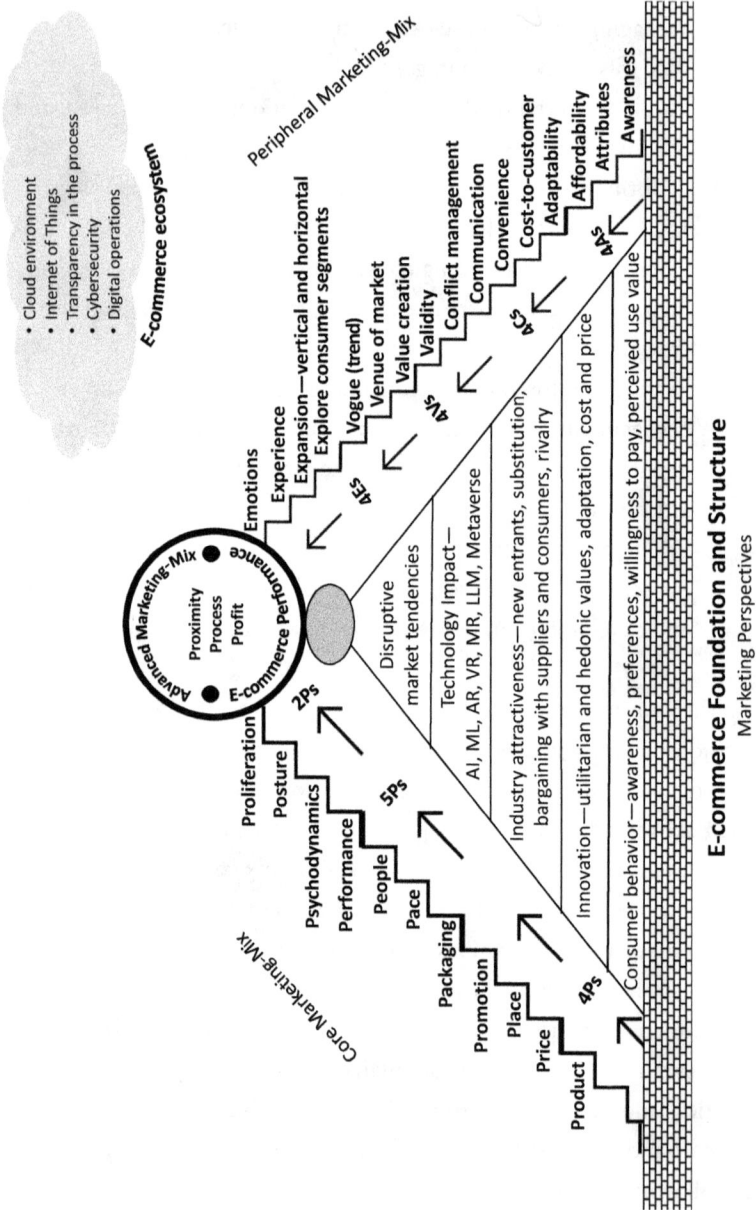

E-commerce ecosystem

- Cloud environment
- Internet of Things
- Transparency in the process
- Cybersecurity
- Digital operations

Peripheral Marketing-Mix

Advanced Marketing-Mix

- Performance
- Proximity
- Process
- Profit
- E-commerce Performance

Core Marketing-Mix

Emotions
Experience
Expansion—vertical and horizontal
Explore consumer segments
Vogue (trend)
Venue of market
Value creation
Validity
Conflict management
Communication
Convenience
Cost-to-customer
Adaptability
Affordability
Attributes
Awareness

4ES
4VS
4CS
4AS

Proliferation
Posture
Psychodynamics
Performance
People
Pace
Packaging
Promotion
Place
Price
Product

2Ps
5Ps
4Ps

Disruptive market tendencies

Technology Impact—AI, ML, AR, VR, MR, LLM, Metaverse

Industry attractiveness—new entrants, substitution, bargaining with suppliers and consumers, rivalry

Innovation—utilitarian and hedonic values, adaptation, cost and price

Consumer behavior—awareness, preferences, willingness to pay, perceived use value

E-commerce Foundation and Structure
Marketing Perspectives

Figure 2.2 Advanced marketing-mix elements

innovation, industry attractiveness, technology impact, and disruptive market tendencies. Advanced marketing-mix strategies help companies sustain oligopolistic competition and manage the threats of market entropy. Staying prepared by taking customers into confidence is one of the effective ways to combat market chaos caused by price competitiveness, low-end competing products of new entrants, substitution effect, and demand fragmentation due to bargaining of consumers and suppliers. Companies need to systematically learn competitors' signals and strategies to understand the market complexity resulting from the various attributes of competition. Organizational learning is also a cognitive process, which entails understanding the array of information, infusing data with right interpretations, and drawing inferences. Commonly, competition information needs to be fragmented and analyzed to learn about competitors' strategy.

Most consumer-centric companies work with dynamic marketing-mix, as often strategies need to be revised either by introducing ad hoc elements of marketing strategies or by laying emphasis on specific marketing-mix elements to develop marketing strategies specific to geodemographic segments. The widespread adoption of marketing technology driving e-commerce trends and leveraging social media to study peer interactions and gather their consumption experiences have dramatically altered the set of products consumers compare before making a purchase decision. Marketing through social channels in the 21st century has succeeded in connecting consumers with companies, brands, and destinations by highlighting peer evaluations, consumer preferences, and motivations toward buying decisions. However, the contribution of marketing technology in establishing both product and customer interconnectedness across markets prompts companies to make the dynamic decision based on market competition trends. Dynamic marketing decisions often result in inconsistencies in consumer policies of the company, and the deliverables of brands are affected (Dass and Kumar 2014).

Marketing-mix adopted by consumer-centric companies is largely technology oriented, as each element of the marketing-mix is configured with requirements of growing marketing technology. Effective use of digital space in business has made e-commerce and m-commerce more popular over conventional telemarketing strategies of the 20th century. Mobile marketing and visual merchandising with the help of online product simulations have boosted product innovation and market competition. Digital marketing approaches have emerged as an increasingly dominant component of firms' overall promotional strategies. The involvement of social media in sharing experiences of consumers has generated strong psychodynamic effects as an intangible tool empowering consumer to govern the performance of products and services. The importance of this element in marketing-mix can be seen as the extent and quality of engagement of consumers on digital platforms, time spent on mobile media, managing consumer forums and participating in public blogs on Internet, number of searches, and direct and indirect referral to promote sales. However, the effectiveness of marketing technology needs to be improved by monitoring the shifts in "consumer-convenience-cost-community" metrics representing the significance of 4Cs in marketing strategies.

Among various e-commerce factors, companies need to periodically evaluate changes in consumer preferences, order bounce rates, add-to-cart rates, shopping cart abandonment, referred decision of consumers, and average order size. Successful e-commerce companies like Amazon, Alibaba, and Flipchart tend to capitalize on the quality of Internet services and consumer connectivity and develop the ability to generate location-sensitive offers. These companies stay connected with consumers by regularly posting relevant personalized messages and offers. However, as web-based marketing technology has almost uprooted brick-and-mortar stores from business, consumer-centric and B-to-B companies need to develop online campaigns and consumer shows to build confidence and sovereignty among stakeholders. In this manner, extrinsic complexity in using digital marketing technologies can be largely resolved (Berman 2016).

The elements of marketing-mix have evolved over the years in reference to changing business environment, shifts in industry focus, and government regulations. The fundamental elements of marketing-mix comprising product, price, place, and promotion still dominate the process of developing marketing strategy. Most successful companies like General Electric, Procter & Gamble, and Cisco believed in developing consumer-centric marketing-mix to enhance market performance of their products and services. An effective marketing-mix actively pushes innovative and unfamiliar brands in the market by making clear passages through competition to serve target markets. Marketers have been aggressive in their pursuit to launch innovation-led products as effective consumer solutions in linking elements of marketing-mix. Managers implementing the marketing-mix often face the challenge of its best fit to the different market environments and consumer expectations. The marketing-mix framework of a company moves in a pyramidal dimension, converging marketing policies of the company, people (intertwining salespeople and consumers), and process (presenting simple and transparent transaction processes to enhance organizational performance) within an organizational system (Comstock et al. 2010).

Core Marketing-Mix—the 11P Factors

Marketing-mix in a company has evolved over the existing business environment and government policies in a destination market. Marketing-mix consists of 11 elements spread across the taxonomic distributions of basic elements (4Ps), extended functional elements (5Ps), and design elements (2Ps) of a company. The basic elements that integrate product, price, place, and promotion elements with varied attributes of each element in this category of marketing-mix are exhibited in Figure 2.2.

Product

Products in the contemporary marketplace are consumer driven and are developed as a solution to consumer needs. The intangible factor of perceived use value and tangible preference of consumers determining the value for money of products govern the consumers' decision-making process for buying the products. Consumer-centric companies like Apple, IKEA, Procter & Gamble, and General Electric consider both design and marketing strategies important tools in creating product preference, perceived use value, and deeper emotional value for consumers. In context of changing global business trends, relationship-based customer management is integrated with product management strategies to drive emotional values among consumers (Noble and Kumar 2008). Companies in the global market generally believe product differentiation appeals to potential consumers who want their needs satisfied over existing product advantages (Flores et al. 2003). As market competition is growing continuously, many products do not move to the mature stage as they are either withdrawn from the market or reintroduced with modifications as second- or new-generation products.

Price

Pricing is one of the most complex decisions facing any company. Along with a lack of academic interest (especially among marketing academics) in the field of pricing, this complexity has contributed to the dominance of simplified, cost-based formulas when levying prices. Price is a sensitive tool for fixing profitability in consumer-centric companies. Every fluctuation in pricing leaves a significant impact on both revenues and profitability of the company. Therefore, ineffective planning in pricing affects the profitability of products and services in a company. In the competitive marketplace, where consumers experience attractive products frequently, they exhibit varied preferences, lean toward dynamic motivations, and show inconsistency in propensity to spend. Accordingly, consumers assign different degrees of emphasis regarding price to determine their purchase decisions (Kohli and Suri 2011).

Place

Place refers to the distribution system of goods and services, and the consumer philosophy of touch, feel, and pick is mostly governed by the availability of products either in virtual or brick-and-mortar stores. Product availability in stores makes consumers product-loyal instead of brand-loyal with instantaneous switching behavior. Hence, to prevent consumers from switching brands, most consumer products companies tend to continuously replenish inventory in retail outlets. Such practice of 360° supplies is attributed to the dynamic distribution management supported by the radio frequency identification (RFID) technology. The RFID technology has driven companies to work with automated distribution process to identify inventory requirements in retail outlets on real-time platforms. The RFID technology has contributed significantly to reduce the transaction costs in supply management, ensure on-time deliveries, control the brand-switching behavior, and increase consumer value. AI and machine learning algorithms are used for demand forecasting, route optimization, and inventory management. These technologies help predict customer demand, optimize delivery routes, and manage stock levels more efficiently. IoT devices, such as sensors and GPS trackers, provide real-time data on the location and condition of goods. This enhances visibility across the supply chain, allowing for better tracking and management of shipments. The blockchain technology ensures transparency and security in the supply chain by providing a tamper-proof record of transactions. This is particularly useful for tracking the provenance of goods and ensuring compliance with regulations

Technology-led distribution strategy has been successful over the years, as it helps companies in minimizing the cost, time, and risk (CTR) effects in managing distribution. Lowering the CTR effects increases consumer value, brand loyalty, market share, and profitability of the company. The distribution management involves social media as a driver of CTR-associated distribution strategy. In this strategy, companies improve customer relationships by developing skills in carefully listening, documenting, and responding to their concerns.

Promotion

The promotional strategies of consumer-centric companies have become a large and growing part of marketing budgets of companies worldwide. Among fashion-oriented brands, promotions are largely driven by word-of-mouth and interactions on social media with other consumers. Promotional strategies are evaluated by companies in reference to its impact on volume of sales, market share, and their contribution to the profit specific to the products and services. Most consumer-centric companies follow three major strategies in promoting the products through advertisements and digital consumer communication: *drive strategy*—through frequent communications in a short span on print or digital channels; *cue strategy*—by inserting product communications in regular intervals on print or electronic media; and *Flanker strategy*—using a prefix and suffix to the brand name exhibiting the new looks and values of the brand. The proximity of digital promotion is enhanced by online and hybrid firms through search engine optimization of website to rank higher in search engine results pages. This increases organic traffic to the company's website by making it more visible to people searching for relevant keywords. Content marketing is one of the dynamic strategies to promote products and services today, which includes creating valuable content such as blog posts, videos, infographics, and eBooks, and helps attract and engage your target audience. Content marketing builds trust and authority, driving long-term customer relationships.

Packaging

Packaging and marketing affect the business performance of production-, sales-, and marketing-led companies. Ergonomics of packaging today plays a significant role in establishing the product attractiveness, developing consumer preferences, defining the market, determining price, and reinforcing the brand values. Innovation in packaging industry is growing strongly to add value to brands and develop unique selling propositions (USPs) for most consumer products companies (Farmer 2012). Technology has significantly advanced in the packaging of both consumer and industrial products. Biodegradable and compostable materials are widely used in the packaging of products such as bioplastics made from plant-based materials and compostable packaging that decomposes in composting conditions, which reduce adverse environmental impact. Firms are encouraged by local regulations to use post-consumer-recycled materials that help reduce waste and reduce the demand for virgin materials. Internet of Packaging is a technological integration in packaging processes, which uses embedded sensors and QR codes in packaging that allow for real-time tracking and interaction. Consumers can scan codes to get product information, check authenticity, and even receive personalized contents. Automated packaging lines include robotics, and automation streamlines the packaging process, increasing efficiency and reducing labor costs. Automated systems can handle tasks like filling, sealing, and labeling with high precision. In addition, 3D printing allows for the creation of customized packaging designs quickly and cost-effectively. This is particularly useful for prototyping and small-batch production. Nanomaterial is also used to improve the strength, barrier properties, and functionality of packaging of climate-sensitive products such as nano-coating that make packaging more resistant to moisture and gases.

Pace—First-Mover Advantage

Etymologically, "pace" indicates consistent and continuous speed in moving things. In the context of business, pace illustrates the marketing strategies that companies deploy to move ahead of their competitors. Most companies in the competitive marketplace struggle to gain first-mover advantage, increase market share, and augment profit. First-mover advantage is a competitive edge that a company gains by being the first to introduce a product or service in a particular market. Being first allows products in a competitive marketplace, in which a firm could build strong brand recognition and customer loyalty ahead of competitors' entry in the market and gain high market share through effective leadership. Moving as a near monopolist, a first-mover firm gains adequate time to develop cost-efficient ways of procuring, manufacturing, or delivering its products, which, in turn, leads to the firm achieving economies of scale and overriding future market competition. Early entrants can secure access to critical resources, such as prime locations, raw materials, and key suppliers, which can be harder for later entrants to obtain. For example, Amazon in the United States and Alibaba in China had tremendous first-mover advantage in e-commerce, which has raised the performance barriers high for other firms that joined the industry later. Customers who adopt the first mover's product may face high switching costs, making them less likely to switch to a competitor later. Firms as first movers also spend more resources to attract consumers and position their brands, which tends to lower the profit rate. However, efficient companies try to minimize the cost, time, and risk (CTR) factors in launching and delivering products in the marketplace. Many companies believe that the first company in a new product category gets a significant breakthrough in the market and gets long-lasting benefits (Rajagopal 2019).

People

People in the marketing-mix constitute front-liners in markets who manage the sale of products and services. Selling is an art largely associated with the behavioral skills of the sale personnel of a sales organization. In a competitive marketplace, selling is performed using scientific methods of product presentation, advertising, and various approaches drawn to take the customer into confidence. A firm begins to sell its products in a competitive marketplace and thrives continuously on acquiring new customers and launches new product lines or services to gain competitive advantage, retain existing customers, enhance customer value, and gain a competitive lead in the market. To compete in a dynamic and interactive marketplace environment, firms must transform their focus from just selling products and services to value-added sales management, in order to maximize customer lifetime value and encourage repeat sales. Hence, firms should ensure that products and services offered by salespeople must be made subservient to customer relationships. New-generation sales management strategies have grown out of basic marketing-mix strategies comprising product, price, place, and promotion. Thus, frontliners' strategies must not only focus on enhancing the volume of sales but must also focus on serving customers for generating long-term customer loyalty. Sales effectiveness is developed through cost-control and the customer value augmentation process. It has been observed that the selling process itself has changed over time, and most firms have adopted customer-centric selling process because of the increase in market competition due to fast penetration of global firms (Rajagopal 2010).

Performance

Performance in the marketing-mix is considered to be a hybrid element. This element evolved through various factors, including all the basic elements of marketing-mix, innovation and continuous improvement, organizational culture, employee engagement, and consumer involvement in cocreating products to enhance consumer value. To thrive in competitive open markets, firms need to map their strategic choices on business performance matrix in reference to various vital variables such as cost, price, innovation, differentiation, distribution, technology, promotion, customer value, and psychodynamics. Firms need to adapt to new roles of low-cost entrants, focused segment marketers, and providers of shared utilities. Competing firms must also be prepared to make new strategic choices as the structure of the industry changes, set clear goals and track key performance indicators, leverage data-driven decision-making, invest in employee development, optimize operational efficiency, build strong customer relationships, implement continuous improvement strategies, and regularly review and benchmark against industry standards.

Psychodynamics

Psychodynamics is a cognitive process of consumers that is induced by digital or personal word-of-mouth and shared use value on products or services among consumers. The psychodynamics on the perceived use value of products or services affect both the conscious and unconscious states of mind, which develops push-and-pull effects in business. It also plays significantly with consumer emotions and crowd behavior toward a brand. Positive psychodynamics among consumers creates a "pull" effect for specific brands in the market. The pull-effect generates high consumer demand that benefits companies in increasing market share and profit by reducing the marketing costs. Such costs for brands are spread across advertisements, in-store promotions, price discounts, and point-of-sales incentives to consumers. Psychodynamics also generate referrals and brand advocacy behavior among consumers, which helps companies acquire new consumers at relatively low cost. Most firms involving social media as a marketing communication channel tap the knowledge and expertise of consumers for mutual benefit and brand-building process more than a traditional knowledge management approach where people dump their information in a giant database that nobody reads. Such firms can create an environment where they go through peer-to-peer collaboration. Emerging firms may initially build very small collaborative tools that enable their peer communication design to kick off the consumer–company collaboration process and to get experience in understanding how it provides mutual benefits (Rajagopal 2013). Psychodynamics helps firms in understanding marketing psychology about how people think and act and how to apply psychological principles to marketing strategies. Digital marketing can use psychological insights to optimize campaigns, ads, and copy to drive purchase behavior by analyzing consumer behavior.

Posture

Posture of the company and its path of business proliferation by diversifying the business operations to new markets and expanding its product portfolio constitute the design elements in the marketing-mix of a company. Corporate image develops the posture of a company within the industry and among the consumers in the marketplace. Consumer confidence is built through the corporate image that develops brand association and brand loyalty among consumers. Most companies are engaged in promoting their internal and external stakeholders to maintain and protect their reputations. To enhance the effects of corporate reputation and unveil a highly promising business face among public, consumer-centric companies communicate their reputation message in the form of a corporate story or as a narrative that speaks about the company's mission, morality, and modes of operation (Dowling 2006). Besides business performance, corporate reputation is earned through delivering more than just financial returns, enhancing value to the stakeholders, and growing as social institutions. Among various facets of institutional growth, a social purpose, long-term focus, emotional engagement, partnering with the public, innovation, and team leadership would help in constructing building blocks of a more sustainable corporate reputation of a company (Kanter 2011). In addition, community engagement, labor relations, environmental protection, corporate governance, and supply chain accountability also help companies to enhance their corporate reputation and create public image to gain competitive advantage.

Proliferation

Proliferation of business activities are commonly developed around product and market diversifications, exploring new consumer segments for existing and future products developed using advanced technologies. Consumer-centric companies planning for business proliferation might face the risk of disruptive innovation and gray market competition. However, business proliferations are often challenging for companies to manage and sustain operational efficiency and profits at the desired levels. Sustained profitable growth requires organic sales growth, competence-based and competence-enhancing growth in the market share, increasing shareholder value, and continuous innovation. Consumer products companies such as General Electric Company, Samsung, and Nike have witnessed that augmented products drive the concept of extended sales mechanism for marketing expansion and product diversification. Product diversification strategy is developed to create awareness among unfamiliar products and markets through (a) concentric diversification (products introduced are related to existing ones in terms of marketing or technology), (b) horizontal diversification (new products are unrelated to existing ones but are sold to the same customers), and (c) conglomerate diversification (products are entirely new).

Peripheral Marketing-Mix Elements

Other than the core marketing-mix factors, there are many elements at the periphery of the core that significantly influences the digital or hybrid marketing strategies. The peripheral marketing consists of 4A, 4C, 4V, and 4E elements.

4A Elements

Consumer awareness is the knowledge and understanding of consumers about their rights and responsibilities as buyers. It also includes information that consumers have about products and services, such as product quality, safety, and pricing. The 4A elements are Awareness, Availability, Adaptability, and Affordability. Most consumers show initial resistance to adapt to new products because of low trust, relative risk, low value for money, and low knowledge. Consumer-centric companies generate consumer awareness through corporate advertisements, user-generated content on social media, and interpersonal sharing of experiences. Upon acquiring awareness on products and brands, consumers develop purchase intentions and look for availability of products in outlets within their reach. With growing competition in the market, availability of products is a sensitive contributor to the company's performance in the market. Consumers look for products in the aisles of retail stores today, and in case of non-availability of the desired products, they tend to switch to other available brands. The consumer philosophy today reveals the tendency of "touch, feel, and pick," beyond the brand loyalty. Therefore, consumer products companies follow a 360° distribution of their products in both retail and wholesale outlets, ensuring round-the-week availability of products to prevent product substitution. At the same time, companies also ensure that their products' prices are competitive and affordable. The adaptability to new products among consumers largely depends on two major concerns—(a) value for money and (b) perceived use value. Successful consumer products companies offer continuous education on new products to develop interest among consumers.

4C Elements

In general, consumer-related elements constitute the 4Cs of the peripheral elements of marketing-mix: Consumer relations, Convenience, Cost to customers, and Consumer conflicts in the marketing of products and services. Successful consumer products companies develop satisfactory relations with consumers during the process of prospecting consumers and providing post-sales services to build consumer confidence. As marketing technology is increasing rapidly, expectations of consumers with a company are also growing up. Hence, most companies develop multiples routes to market to provide shopping convenience to consumers. Rapid expansion of e-commerce, m-commerce, and the telemarketing practices of consumer products companies offer competitive shopping conveniences to consumers, such as online product simulations, comparative market panorama, same-day delivery of products, and quick logistics for returns or exchange of products. However, cost-to-consumer is a sensitive determinant of managing consumers within marketing-mix strategies. Cost-to-consumer includes both tangible (price and risk factors) and intangible (time, opportunity cost, and perceived value) costs. Companies manage tangible costs by offering competitive prices and low-risk products to augment consumer value. To implement tangible cost strategies, most consumer products companies like Nestlé and Proctor and Gamble refine cost-cutting capabilities by economizing the consumer offers (get more and spend less). Value-conscious consumers demand cost-innovative pricing approaches in mass markets in both developed and emerging markets. Competitive consumer products companies, therefore, enter into alliances with emerging Chinese companies to gain cost-innovation capabilities and deliver high consumer value (Williamson and Zeng, 2009).

Managing consumer conflicts is a major challenge for consumer products companies, as it is based more on cognitive platforms than on the inefficiencies related to tangible product and services. Consumer conflicts commonly emerge due to incongruence between consumers' needs and the attributes of products; incompatibility of services and consumer relations; differences in consumer perceptions, attitudes, and values; and social influence on consumer behavior. Relating these conditions to the unique characteristics of services, such as intangibility, heterogeneity, and coproduction, suggests that many products and services are likely to generate conflict between manufacturing companies, service providers, and consumers. However, companies improve customer relations practices and cocreate peer-driven approaches to manage such consumer conflicts.

4V Elements

The marketing performance of companies is also affected by the 4V's comprising the Value perceptions of consumers, peer Validity, Venue and shopping experience, and Vogue exhibited in the market. The sharing of consumer experiences on social media provides validation to consumer perceptions and expectations on products and services. Customer value is complex and intangible to measure. It is about how much a customer perceives a product or service is worth to them. The value perception is the net difference between the benefits a customer receives from a product or service and the costs they invest in obtaining it. Common marketing approaches that help firms create customer value include the following attributes:

- The end-use price, which the consumer pays for the product or service;
- The price–quality relationship, which affects the value-for-money concept and emotions of the consumer;
- Benefits offered by the firm to market the products—the benefits the customer receives from the product or service—such as advantages of ownership, image, and access to a solution—do help in building overall customer satisfaction and loyalty perceptions;

- Value perception critically affects the emotional values of consumer and explains the intangible benefits the customer receives from the product or service.

Consequently, customer value is the perceived worth of a product or service in the eyes of the customer. Measuring customer value, firms can understand the practical or utilitarian aspects of a product or service, such as its features, performance, reliability, and analyze the neurobehavioral feelings or psychological benefits a customer experiences, such as satisfaction, trust, and brand loyalty.

4E Elements

The 4Es in the marketing-mix are associated with the sharing of consumer experiences on social media and digital space and development of perceptions led by emotions on brands. These elements allow companies to develop strategies for exploring and expanding business in new geodemographic segments and exploiting the markets by catering the demand to the fullest extent possible. Besides several 4-factor peripheral elements of marketing-mix, VRINE framework is an extended business model that analyzes the capabilities and competencies of a marketing organization and its brands for sustainable growth in competitive marketplace. VRINE framework refers to Value, Rarity, Inimitability, Non-substitutability, and Exploitability of brands. The most successful companies do not just market good products through strong distribution systems; they also develop a deep understanding of customers. Such business integration requires lots of cocreated insights on marketing. Accordingly, firms develop a set of marketing policies, implementable strategies, associate people, and processes that can translate the marketing philosophy of the business organizations into efficient actionable strategies to gain competitive advantage.

Virtual Supply Chain

Advancement of ICT helps online business firms to transform conventional supply chain into a virtual supply chain (VSC) and render their logistics management as a digital representation of a physical supply chain. It is essentially a computer-based model that allows businesses to visualize and manage the entire network of suppliers, manufacturers, distributors, and warehouses in real-time, enabling better decision-making by simulating different operational scenarios. VSC enables firms to identify potential issues before they occur in the actual supply chain, as this computer-aided supply chain and logistics model relies heavily on data-sharing and advanced technologies to create a flexible and responsive network. VSC model mirrors the physical supply chain, allowing for analysis and optimization without needing to physically manipulate inventory and logistics. VSC improves business operations by providing a seamless flow of data between all supply chain partners, enabling real-time visibility into inventory levels, production schedules, and delivery status. Data-based improved decision-making is enabled in the VSC model; by simulating different scenarios, businesses can identify potential disruptions and make proactive adjustments to their supply chain.

VSC represents data visualization of manufacturing plants and warehouses along with supply chain components of the extended enterprise—customers, suppliers, logistics providers, and other related players in the online supply chain process. VSC provides supply chain planners an overall view of operations as well as the ability to zoom in on various areas of interest. Besides Enterprise Resource Planning (ERP) and customized supply chain project planning, monitoring, and evaluation platforms used by firms, many underlying challenges can be avoided by having a platform with cloud-based solution that is independent of the systems and hardware at the individual organizations. Thus, VSC is a cloud-based system that connects to the IT system of company at the backend. This system enables companies to manage the supply chain process in decentralized departments of a single unit rather than in separate, disjointed entities. Such functional integration enhances planning functions, reduces inefficiencies, eliminates surprises, and provides end-to-end visibility and transparency in operations in real-time leading to effective communication and coordination in the VSC process.

VSC embeds a digital-twin perspective—a virtual model of a physical product, process, or system. In the context of supply chains, it replicates the entire supply chain network, including manufacturing plants, warehouses, suppliers, and logistics providers. AI and machine learning algorithms analyze data to predict demand, optimize routes, and identify potential disruptions. These technologies help in making informed decisions quickly. Blockchain technology ensures transparency and security in VSC by providing a tamper-proof record of transactions. This is particularly useful for tracking the provenance of goods and ensuring compliance with regulations.

Case Study

CS1 *Alibaba E-commerce System*

Amidst the globally transcending ICT, Alibaba emerged as a Chinese multinational technology company in 1999 with specialization in e-commerce, retail, and technology services. The company operates a group of enterprises in the online marketplace, which include Alibaba.com (e-commerce), AliExpress.com (D-to-C), Taobao (C-to-C), and Tmall (Greater China e-commerce of branded products). In all, Alibaba e-commerce group has various business operations that bring together businesses and consumers with manufacturers, wholesalers, and retailers. Alibaba offers financial services such as wealth management and micro-loans through its digital payment platform known as Alipay, which serves as a digital wallet and payment app that allows users to make payments online, in-person, and through the mobile application. The mother company (Alibaba) also offers cloud computing services, including cloud servers, Elastic Compute Service (ECS), CloudBox, Compute Nest, and more cloud-based services. Alibaba's business model focuses on coordinating the functions associated with retail into a network of manufacturers, sellers, marketers, and other service providers by synchronizing with the customer preferences, buying, and value creation.

AliExpress is an online marketplace that allows consumers to buy products directly from manufacturers and distributors in China and other countries since 2010. The company sells a wide variety of products, including clothing, electronics, sporting goods, beauty and health items, jewelry, computers, cellphones, and home appliances. It encourages products of small businesses of China and Southeast Asian region by gaining competitive edge with low prices to attract customers. AliExpress has become a global marketplace today targeting consumers around the world and enabling them to buy directly from manufacturers and distributors in

China and around the world, including in the United States, Brazil, Russia, and other big emerging markets. AliExpress started as a B-to-B buying and selling portal. It has since expanded to include B-to-C, C-to-C, cloud computing, and payment services. As of 2016, AliExpress ran websites in English, Spanish, Korean, Dutch, French, Italian, German, Polish, Turkish, Portuguese, Indonesian, Russian, Ukrainian, Vietnamese, Japanese, Thai, and other languages—English being the default offered to those countries with languages outside the preceding list. AliExpress is often used by e-commerce stores that use a drop-ship business model. A *drop-shipping* business model is an online retail method where a seller takes customer orders but maintains zero inventory by linking third-party suppliers (3PS) to deliver the products ordered by the customers. When a customer purchases a product, the seller buys it from a third-party supplier who then directly ships the item to the customer, essentially allowing the seller to market and sell products without managing physical inventory.

Taobao came to existence in 2003 as a leading Chinese online shopping platform; it is considered the biggest C-to-C retail marketplace in China, where individuals and small businesses can sell their products directly to customers through their own online stores on the platform. Taobao is owned by the Alibaba Group and is often referred to as the *Amazon of China*. Taobao marketplace facilitates C-to-C retail selling by providing a platform for small businesses and individual entrepreneurs to open online stores that mainly cater to consumers in Chinese-speaking regions and across the Southeast Asia region, and payments can be made via online accounts. Its stores usually offer an express delivery service. Sellers can post goods for sale either through a fixed price or an auction. Auctions make up a small percentage of transactions, whereas most of the products are new merchandise sold at fixed prices. Taobao users usually read feedback and compare items from multiple shops. Taobao's popular payment platform is Alibaba's Alipay—a digital wallet. Taobao beta-launched e-Tao as an independent search engine for online shopping to provide merchant information from several major consumer e-commerce websites in China. Online shoppers can use the site to compare prices across sellers. According to the Alibaba Group website, e-Tao offers products from Amazon China, Dangdang, Gome, Yihaodian, Nike China and Vancl, as well as Taobao and Tmall.

Alipay has emerged as one of the popular payment platforms in China with increasingly active users in China, and the coverage of Alipay digital wallet is expanding internationally. The mobile payment app is owned by Ant Group (an affiliate company of the Alibaba Group, which owns AliExpress). Alipay supports multiple payment methods, including credit cards, debit cards, and bank transfers. Users can store their card details in the app and make payments using their phone. This digital wallet uses advanced encryption technology and a real-time risk-monitoring system to keep customers data safe from any cyber-attacks.

Despite the integration of several e-commerce companies to serve the required business activities, Alibaba Group has complex challenges facing it. The regulatory and geopolitical issues have major implications for cross-border and overseas e-commerce operations, including in terms of trade and delivery for customers located in the United States and in the European region. Alibaba faces ongoing regulatory scrutiny in China, which has impacted its operations and market performance. Additionally, geopolitical tensions between the United States and China have created uncertainties, particularly affecting its cloud computing business. On the technology front, the company is facing concerns about the stability and future direction of Alibaba's cloud business due to change in leadership. However, despite exhibiting growth in some areas, the company is experiencing profitability challenges and a decline in cash flow.

Alibaba faces intense competition from other tech giants like Amazon, JD.com, and Pinduoduo, which puts pressure on its market share and growth potential. The decision to cancel the spin-off of its cloud computing unit due to U.S. rules on advanced chips has led to significant drops in stock value and added to investor apprehensions. Nonetheless, Alibaba continues to push forward with its AI-driven growth strategies and international expansion efforts. Addressing these issues will be crucial for Alibaba to regain investor confidence and sustain its growth.

Summary

This chapter focuses on the strategic (long-term) virtual business modeling using advanced e-commerce designs, e-commerce ecosystem, and advanced marketing-mix comprising 27 core and peripheral elements overshadowing the conventional 4Ps of product, price, place, and promotions. Virtual businesses targeting the B-to-C segment are engaged in selling consumer products directly to their end-users. The decision-making process for online purchase is very agile, and the purchase information can be stored in the customer account with the e-commerce company. E-commerce has another growing segment—industrial marketing, also known as B-to-B marketing, which involves the marketing of goods and services from one business to another. The rise of m-commerce engaging customers through mobile apps and social media channels has significantly boosted the popularity of C-to-C e-commerce, making it easier for consumers to buy and sell items without territorial boundaries. In addition, the click-and-collect or online-to-offline (O-to-O) marketing, often abbreviated as O-to-O, refers to a marketing strategy where businesses use online channels like websites and social media to attract customers to make purchases in their physical stores, essentially bridging the gap between digital and physical shopping experiences. The notion of business ecosystem addresses the relative concepts of collaboration and competition, such as customer-centric and market-led strategies of business in both predetermined and dynamic business systems. This chapter discusses contemporary marketing philosophy, explaining it with the analogy of a polyhedron framework that has a triangular prismatic effect with five faces, six edges, and nine vertices. The philosophical thoughts on modern business can be stretched wide from the geometric structure to the functional propositions in the marketplace, which entails broadly the market, society, and customer values.

It is argued in the chapter that the advanced marketing-mix has 11Ps comprising the conventional 4Ps as product, price, place, and promotion and the other 7Ps modulate the contemporary marketing decisions. The new 5Ps including packaging, pace (competitive dynamics), people (front-liners in marketing), performance, and psychodynamics (peer-to-peer, word-of-mouth, or the grapevine effect) constitute the extended operational factors of marketing-mix. The additional 2Ps are known as corporate factors that involve posture (corporate image) and proliferation (product and market diversification). The peripheral marketing consists of 4A, 4C, 4V, and 4E elements. This chapter also argues that the VSC improves business operations with seamless flow of data between all supply chain partners, enabling real-time visibility into inventory levels, production schedules, and delivery status. Data-based improved decision-making is enabled in the VSC model; by simulating different scenarios, businesses can identify potential disruptions and make proactive adjustments to their supply chain. This chapter discusses also the business canvas–marketing modeling fit to improve the performance of virtual marketing. Emerging trends on VSC management and their integration with the virtual business modeling has been in discussed in the chapter. A major challenge for e-commerce is how to connect people to business in the cyber–physical engagement of consumers and behavioral proximity emphasizing the role of interactive marketing on cyberspace with the support of ICT, which constituted the core discussion in this chapter. Discussions conclude with a case study of Alibaba e-commerce company endorsing the points that are central to this chapter.

References

Berman, B. 2016. "Planning and Implementing Effective Mobile Marketing Programs." *Business Horizons* 59 (4): 431–9.

Comstock, B., R. Gulat, and S. Liguori. 2010. "Unleashing the Power of Marketing." *Harvard Business Review* 88 (10): 90–8.

Dass, M., and S. Kumar. 2014. "Bringing Product and Consumer Ecosystems to the Strategic Forefront." *Business Horizons* 57 (2): 225–34.

Dowling, G. R. 2006. "Communicating Corporate Reputation Through Stories." *California Management Review* 49 (1): 82–100.

Farmer, N. 2012. *Packaging and Marketing*. Packaging Technology. Cambridge, UK: Woodhead Publishing.

Flores, F., M. F., Letelier, and C. Spinosa. 2003. "Developing Productive Customers in Emerging Markets." *California Management Review* 45 (4): 77–103.

Kanter, R. M. 2011. "How Great Companies Think Differently." *Harvard Business Review* 89 (11): 66–78.

Kohli, C., and R. Suri. 2011. "The Price is Right? Guidelines for Pricing to Enhance Profitability." *Business Horizons* 54 (6): 563–73.

Noble, C. H., and M. Kumar. 2008. "Using Product Design Strategically to Create Deeper Consumer Connections." *Business Horizons* 51 (5): 441–50.

Parente, R. C., J. M.G. Geleilate, and K. Rong. 2018. "The Sharing Economy Globalization Phenomenon: A Research Agenda." *Journal of International Management* 24 (1): 52–64.

Rajagopal. 2011. "The Symphony Paradigm: Strategy for Managing Market Competition." *Journal of Transnational Management* 16 (3): 181–99.

Rajagopal. 2010. *Sales Dynamics: Thinking Outside the Box.* Hauppauge: Nova Science Publishers Inc.

Rajagopal. 2013. *Managing Social Media and Consumerism: The Grapevine Effect in Competitive Markets.* Basingstoke, UK: Palgrave Macmillan.

Rajagopal. 2019. *Contemporary Marketing Strategy: Analyzing Consumer Behavior to Drive Managerial Decision-Making.* Cham, Switzerland: Springer (A Palgrave Macmillan Imprint).

Rajagopal. 2024. *Proximity Marketing: Converging Community, Consciousness, and Consumption.* Business Expert Press.

The Business Model Analyst. 2023. "Etsy Business Model." Accessed November 16, 2024. https://businessmodelanalyst.com/etsy-business-model/.

Williamson, P. J., and M. Zeng 2009. "Value-for-Money Strategies for Recessionary Times." *Harvard Business Review* 87 (3): 66–74.

CHAPTER 3

Seamless Technology

Overview

The seamless ambience of virtual business technology has grown in the 21st century. Its spread across IoT, Metaverse Reality (MR), and beyond AR and VR is discussed in this chapter. The contemporary tools to develop techno-biz models in specific sectors such as consumer health and well-being, electronic home appliances, fashion, value, and lifestyle products are also discussed. This chapter provides an e-commerce website development blueprint that guides new entrepreneurs in managing e-commerce business. In addition, the chapter also discusses concepts such as virtual block chains, technology infrastructure, and consumer–firm virtual engagement. Discussions on the innovating virtual marketing practices and push-pull effects support the conversations on techno-biz modeling in this chapter. Arguments and critical discussions in this chapter also include the long-term (strategic) versus short-term (tactical) impact of virtual marketing on the competitiveness and performance of customer-centric businesses (Juntunen et al. 2019). Discussions on developing the technology-led e-commerce strategy to gain competitiveness and converge virtual marketing approaches with customer value are spread across all chapters in the book.

Architecting E-commerce

Architecting an effective e-commerce firm, complying with the requirements of technology infrastructure, is very essential besides identifying target audience, analyzing existing market competition, setting up clear goals, choosing the right suppliers, and choosing appropriate marketing channels. As e-commerce is all about user-efficient buying platforms, virtual store displays, order processing, and delivery management, it is important for firms to optimize their e-commerce websites for search engines through the search engine optimization (SEO) process. SEO efficiency can be enhanced by adding relevant keywords, meta descriptions, and structured data to improve search efficacy and search engine ranking. Efficient B-to-C websites must be able to create compelling product pages, streamline the checkout process, implement personalized marketing tactics, and track results to make necessary adjustments. The key aspects of e-commerce strategy include defining ways of brand positioning, pricing, promotions, and customer acquisition methods while leveraging social media and e-mail marketing to engage audience and reinforce their buying intentions. With radical changes in consumer preferences due to disruptive technologies and frugal innovations, it is often challenging for e-commerce firms to understand consumer demographics, needs, buying behaviors, and online buying behavior. Analyzing competitive strategies is another underlying challenge, and firms must conduct research on the websites of competing e-commerce firms' pricing, visual merchandising, and marketing strategies to develop differential marketing strategies to gain competitive advantage. Defining product-mix (product categories and product line), competitive features, quality, pricing, and positioning within the market enables firms to create a consistent brand image across all platforms, including logo, messaging, and tone of voice, which also helps in developing virtual brand identity. Nonetheless, a clean, intuitive website layout with easy navigation and quick loading time attracts online buyers and enables them to navigate across the various departments of the store to make appropriate buying decisions. Developing high-quality product pages including detailed product descriptions, high-resolution images, customer reviews, and clear size/color options encourages visual merchandising and improves the performance of e-commerce.

E-commerce Infrastructure

The foundation of an online business is the state-of-the art technology infrastructure, which provides the tools and systems needed to run a virtual store. It includes the hardware, software, and services that support the e-commerce business and enables an integrated function of e-commerce operations to ensure smooth operations and a seamless customer experience.

One of the principal frameworks of e-commerce infrastructure is the webserver architecture that includes servers engaged to host websites, manage operating systems, store content, and handle data transmission to users. Therefore, webservers are the lifeline of e-commerce and are crucial for maintaining the overall performance and reliability of the e-commerce operational system. Designing webservers for e-commerce firms involves several critical considerations to ensure online stores perform fast, secure, and scalable buying and selling operations. The requirement for the right webservers to support the inflow and outflow of products, processes, and services needs evaluating the current and future resource requirements, traffic projections, and budgeting. This helps firms in choosing the right server specifications. While setting up servers for a basic low-profile e-commerce firm, the website specifications that ensure performance, security, and scalability need the following specifications:

- Main Frame Computer
  - For basic e-commerce sites: At least a quad-core processor (e.g., 4 x 1.6 GHz CPUs)
  - For larger sites with higher traffic: More powerful processors, such as 8-core or higher
- RAM
  - Minimum: 4 GB for small sites
  - Recommended: 8 GB or more for medium-to-large sites to handle higher traffic and more complex operations
- Storage
  - SSDs (Solid-State Drives) are preferred for faster read/write speeds
  - Minimum: 10 GB for database storage
  - Recommended: 50 GB or more, depending on the size of your product catalog and user data
- Bandwidth
  - Ensure sufficient bandwidth to handle peak traffic times without slowdowns
  - Consider scalable options if using cloud hosting to adjust based on demand

- Database
  - MySQL version 5.7 or greater, or MariaDB version 10.4 or greater
  - Ensure the database server has enough resources to handle queries efficiently
- Operating System (Himel 2023)
  - Linux distributions (e.g., Ubuntu, CentOS) are commonly used for their stability and security
  - Ensure compatibility with your e-commerce platform and other software
- Webserver Software
  - Apache or Nginx are popular choices for their performance and flexibility
  - Ensure proper configuration for handling e-commerce traffic and security
- Security
  - SSL/TLS certificates for secure data transmission
  - Regular security updates and patches
  - Firewalls and intrusion detection/prevention systems
- Backup and Recovery
  - Regular automated backups
  - A robust disaster recovery plan to minimize downtime in case of failures
- Additional Features (Woo, n.d.)
  - Support for HTTPS
  - PHP version 7.4 or greater
  - WordPress memory limit of 256 MB or greater if using WooCommerce.

Startup e-commerce companies or a group of e-commerce companies may choose to share hosting of the webserver with the principal server of the mother company. However, Virtual Private Server (VPS) provides better control over data exchanges in business and resources as compared to the shared hosting for single client firms. Beyond the options discussed above, a dedicated server offers maximum control and resources, which is ideal for large e-commerce sites with heavy traffic. Another option for the webserver is cloud hosting, which is both scalable and flexible, allowing firms to adjust resources based on demand and manage fluctuations in traffic and transactions. While setting up the webserver for e-commerce, most firms face a major challenge to prioritize securities to safely handle sensitive customer data and protect personal data from security breach and cyber-attacks. By implementing SSL certificates, firewalls, and regular security updates, using secured payment gateways, and complying with industry standards like Payment Card Industry Data Security Standard (PCI-DSS), data can be largely protected. PCI-DSS is a set of security standards designed to ensure that all e-commerce firms who accept, process, store, or transmit credit card information maintain a secure environment. This security measure helps in encrypting the transmission of cardholder data across open public networks. In addition to securing the electronic payment processes, firms also need to strengthen the inventory management system to track stock levels, manage orders, and optimize warehouse operations. Efficient inventory management is essential for meeting customer demand and minimizing costs. The shipping and fulfillment solutions manage the logistics of delivering products to customers. These solutions integrate with various carriers and provide real-time tracking to ensure timely and accurate deliveries. Server efficiency can be optimized through the following functional enhancements:

- Content Delivery Network (CDN) enables distribution of content across multiple servers worldwide, reducing load times for users regardless of their location.
- Server-side caching helps to store frequently accessed data, reducing the load on your server and speeding up response times.
- Load balancing distributes incoming traffic across multiple servers to ensure no single server is overwhelmed, improving reliability and performance.

Periodic data backup on other servers prevents system crash and provides the scope for quick recovery of data. In addition, continuously monitoring server performance and security and periodically tracking the server health, load times, and potential vulnerabilities can be managed through regular maintenance (removing bugs, redundant files, and overshadowed space, and carrying out due update) to keep the server functioning smoothly.

Visualization

Visual merchandising in e-commerce is all about displaying products, features, reviews, and visual effects like action images and videos in a way that engages and persuades potential customers. To create visualization impact, every product in a category should have a homepage, which should be able to showcase window display of new products, bestsellers, and promotions to grab attention. In addition, the product homepage must also showcase recommended products matching the attributes of products and consumer search intentions. Showcasing recommended products can be based on generative artificial intelligence (AI) and consumer navigation data analytics. Using algorithmic model supported by AI and machine learning to suggest products based on a customer's browsing and purchase history can increase customer interaction and engagement with products in the virtual merchandising ecosystem. Displaying complementary products together, like how outfits are displayed on mannequins in store, inspires customers to buy more than one item. Optimizing site layout to effectively showcase products is helpful to customers to conduct targeted navigation during the shopping journey. The intuitive navigation and personalized layouts enhance user experience in online shopping and reinforce their interest in staying with the e-commerce website. High-quality imagery and videos enhance consumer experience with products as use of sharp, clear photos and videos stimulate the purchase intention of consumers and reinforce their buying decision. Showcasing products from 360° builds confidence, transparency, and trust on products among consumers. Table 3.1 illustrates various factors associated with the visualization of products on e-commerce platforms.

Developing effective data visualization for e-commerce platforms requires customization of both product's and consumers' information. The product visualization with preferential attributes of the products as suggested by consumers will be more appealing than developing visualization based on merely product features. E-commerce needs visualization of

Table 3.1 Factors influencing product visualization in E-commerce

Linear path	Strategy options	Key elements	Visual taxonomy
• Develop consumer survey • Prepare datasets • Refine your data • Create graphics and charts	• Semantics • Storyboard • Cause and effect (PNS factors)	• Purpose • Contents • Structure • Format • Design	• Decorative • Representative • Mnemonic • Organizational • Relational • Transformational • Interpretive visuals

products based on consumer preferences to build self-image congruence with product features and displays. Such visualization on e-commerce platforms enables neurobehavioral stimulation, emotions, and purchase intentions among consumers. To customize visualization of products on e-commerce platforms, firms must collect data of consumer choices about verbal and nonverbal content, use values, price, process, promotion, customer reviews, colors, images, videos, and the like. Firms can prepare databases and update them periodically to create website graphics and charts using static or animation tools. Data visualization for e-commerce is fundamentally a graphical representation of product and consumer information. By using visual elements like charts, graphs, and maps, data visualization tools provide an accessible way to see and understand trends, outliers, and patterns in data. Data visualization helps in exhibiting complex information in an organized way. Some of the benefits that e-commerce may gain with data visualization are as discussed below:

• Developing sales dashboards to exhibit product performance and track sales performance, revenue, and growth over time.
• Developing customer journey maps to provide confidence to consumers in decision-making and buying process. By visualizing the steps, customers can get into the chronological emotions from their first visit to purchase.
• Conversion funnels as visualization images illustrate the stages of the customer journey and identify the earlier drop-off points, trends, and vulnerability in consumer behavior.

- One of the popular data visualizations methods is the heatmapping method to show how users interact with the e-commerce website. The heatmaps can be created by highlighting popular areas of information, potential interests, and conflict zones.

Visualizing the data allows for rapid interpretation helping the businesses to quickly identify trends and patterns and helps with improved decision-making by presenting data visually. Through effective visualization process, e-commerce firms can make customer-centric decisions based on their preferences and actionable insights. Visual tools can help firms to analyze enhanced customer behavior, preferences, and purchasing patterns, which also provides opportunity for e-commerce firms to compile and display competitor data for effective strategic planning. In addition, interactive charts and infographics can enhance user experience on e-commerce.

To develop visualization on interrelated products and services, e-commerce firms should create semantics of core products like apple. The semantics of apple can be apple juice, apple jam, apple dehydration, organic apple orchards, ethnic farming, apple vinegar, apple sider, and the like. Such semantics will help the firm to identify the related products, processes, sustainability, and the associated ethnicity to display specific varieties of products and attract consumers to navigate on the website. Semantics is fundamentally a study of meanings and etymologies in language that explores how words, phrases, sentences, and texts convey meaning and build contextual relationships. Semantics examines the meaning of words and how these meanings combine to form the meanings of sentences and larger texts; this involves understanding senses and references in the relationship between expressions and the products they refer to. For example, *good health* and *natural product* both refer to the apple but have different senses and consumer perceptions. Semantics is a crucial field in linguistics but can be networked to visualize the business through AI and information technology tools to help firms understand how language works to communicate effectively in customer-centric marketing perspectives.

Creating a storyboard is an attractive way to visualize products on e-commerce platform and develop a webpage for each product within the product category. Visibility of product promotion improves if each product has a storyboard. The outline of storyboard should have the main plot points, characters, and settings related to products. This will serve as the foundation for the storyboard. Images, videos, sketches, and captions related to products help in synchronizing the product visualization to attract consumers and navigators on the e-commerce platform. The story can be divided into sequential scenes or moments that represent a key part of the narrative. Once the rough sketches or images are placed in a sequential order, elements like characters, captions, key actions, movements, transitions, and background music can be set. Finally, to exhibit a storyboard, organize the placeholders with contents in a sequence that makes sense for a product's story on the e-commerce website.

Data visualization has some key elements including clear purpose, attractive content including competitive advantages and use values associated with the products, structure of the visualization framework, organized sequential format to arrange placeholders with comments, and neural design that could inculcate emotions and stimuli among consumers and liberal website navigators. Among many decorative, representative, mnemonic, organizational, relational, transformational, and interpretive visuals for the core categories, mnemonic visuals are images or diagrams used to help the user remember the information by associating it with visual cues. These tools are particularly effective for people to learn from visuals and develop perceptions and can help recall information to support contextual decision-making. Mnemonic visuals work by linking an image with the information you need to remember. For example, to remember the number 8, consumers (particularly children) might visualize a snowman, as the shape resembles the number. Such visual effects facilitate easy navigation on e-commerce websites for consumers of all ages.

E-commerce platforms displaying fashion apparel can be successful with user-friendly technology by optimizing the information at a single click. Virtual retailers of fashion products need to understand shoppers' perspective for personalizing 3D store atmospherics (Ha et al. 2007). Though consumers enjoy browsing products, they might lose interest if navigation becomes complex and non-suggestive to explore identical or similar products. Firms engaged in marketing fashion apparel through virtual platforms need to ensure display of varieties and arraying of products to facilitate easy search with no time limits for making buying decisions. Hurrying consumers to make buying decisions and time-bound canceling of shopping carts not only cause dissatisfaction but also build distrust toward the brand. Product attractiveness should be the primary concern for retailers to build their virtual stores, which also matters to consumers in navigating the products. Navigational support can be enhanced by displaying suggestive products with visual endorsements (videos) to develop awareness, comprehension, conviction, and action among consumers engaged in virtual shopping. The anthropomorphic emotions can be developed by retailers through celebrity endorsements, consumer-oriented videos, and social voices. Virtual retailers should consider modularization of displaying, arraying, and recommending contextual products by similar design, color, size, fashion trends, seasonality, and perceived use values. The anthropomorphic emotions contribute to self-actualization and self-esteem, which helps consumers in non-conflictive decision-making. Virtual retailers should also develop online simulators based on anthropometric data of consumers to drive visual stimulus and help them in experiencing the body image congruence with apparels. Firms retailing fashion apparel online should also be engaged in developing user-generated content through communications on social media encouraging experiential videos, slogans, and reviews. In addition, retailing firms also need to conduct data-text mining to learn about consumer experiences posted on discrete platforms like micro-blogs (Rajagopal and Rajagopal 2023).

Visual Effects and Proximity

The mainstream retailing industry has transformed from traditional shopping practices to multichannel retailing by developing retail business through e-commerce platforms. Such transformation in retailing technology has increased the global market outreach and online penetration of potential customers with increased visual satisfaction and ease-of-use of technology. The visualization features have allowed retailers to demonstrate the 3D store effect by allowing multiple presentations supported by visual technologies to provide sensory perceptions (Zha et al. 2022). Virtual merchandising blended with virtual store ergonomics, product dimensions, and sensory experience tends to instantly substitute the need for physical inspection such as fitness trials, touching, and appearance satisfaction. Effective merchandise display helps shoppers to coordinate a cross-product mix and develop purchase intentions. Visual merchandising stimulates self-image congruence, ontological reasoning, and neurobehavioral outcomes leading to perceptual stimuli and satisfaction reinforcing the feeling of *seeing is experiencing*. The positive attitude toward seeing, believing, and experiencing leads to a decision-making phenomenon within the perceptual triangle of elements comprising knowing, experiencing, and being. Virtual merchandising through clear arraying of product portfolios and simultaneous display of contextual products has given a wide range of options to consumers and supports buying decisions and enables business model innovation among digital retail competitors (Mostaghel et al. 2022). One of the major impacts of digital technologies has been toward 3V factors comprising value creation, value delivery, and value capture. Artificial intelligence (AI) and virtual reality (VR) support consumer learning process on product design, attributes, and values, and this helps consumers make appropriate buying decisions quickly. In addition to AI and VR, chatbots and robot-driven responses enhance consumer experience online and support consumer perceptions on *seeing is experiencing*.

The fusion of conventional communication, brick-and-mortar shopping behavior, and community interactions with technology-led virtual shopping experiences has encouraged consumers to attain a holistic experience of virtual merchandising and an integrated buying experience. Virtual communications supported by enhanced products information, real-time prices, customization advise, order and delivery tracking, and information on purchased transactions have supported consumer perceptions and purchase intentions on various retail technology platforms (Riegger et al. 2021). Fashion apparel is effectively promoted on social media mainly targeting Twitter (now X), Facebook, Instagram, and Tik-Tok through emoticons, social speech tags, and unigrams and bigrams linguistic tags. The virtual display mannequins with anthropomorphic dimensions presenting a human-like musculoskeletal morphology attract consumers to explore the array of products on virtual retail sites to make instant purchase decisions. In addition, embedded videos of models anchoring vogue products on virtual retailing websites stimulate appearance similarity, physical congruence, and social consciousness among consumers to inculcate purchase intentions (Song and Kim 2020).

Customer-centric companies can be engaged in providing information literacy by accelerating vertical (within a specific market) and horizontal (across geodemographic segments in new destinations) expansion to enhance social proximity. By stimulating the consumers to share their prolonged experience on social platforms and analyzing their cognitive feelings, firms can architect the EYE model of proximity marketing, which comprises empowerment, yearning, and emotions. Empowering consumers to lead and manage interactive information forums on products, competition, corporate policies, and PNS factors contributes to the expansion of customer proximity, outreach, and value perceptions (POV). Localized forums can culminate in a regional and global forum. LEGO forums and handicrafts forums in India follow such communication hierarchy, where local artisans interact with the institutional forum to refine their design-thinking concepts and processes. Such an upward movement drives POV and offers them the opportunity to put forth their point of view as well. The proximity metrics can be analyzed by the firms by measuring the input and output time of processing visual communications, information decomposition effects (number of views and extent of information entropy), and information effectiveness to proximity. Cognitive reasoning at the individual and social level helps firms in analyzing social consciousness and sensitivity in consolidating perceptions of people on categorical interactions across social domains, interest groups, and information leads. Proximity technology has transformed physical interactions with digital platforms, which attracts sensory perceptions through visualization, visual proximity, and inculcating the sense of knowing, feeling, and being. Hybridity in information systems and social robotics has significantly contributed to indoctrinating the wisdom of "nudge, feel, and analyze" into crowd information or collective intelligence, which is pivotal in building proximity between people, society, and the firm (Rajagopal 2024).

The phenomenon of *seeing is experiencing* is founded on the maxims of visual perceptions, which leads to cognitive reasoning and developing perceptions on visual objects. The visual data are analyzed within internal neural space, form perceptual images, and drive cognitive reasoning through perceptual motions. The theories of visual perceptions argue that visual objects are perceived through neural networks and cognitive brain imaging to develop contextual semantics and decision-making by subjects. Visual perceptions are often sensitive to judgments, as inadequate construction of visual scenarios generates a gap between cognitive actualization and deception. Visual perceptions are affected by the quality of construction of visual scenario, cognitive inhibition, speed of visuals, and the combination of verbal (dynamic text) and nonverbal (contextual image, color, music, graphics, and appearance of anchors) elements. The scientific development on theory of visual perceptions has indicated several neural space dynamisms in mapping visual perceptions through visual pathways, optic tract, and topographical images (Jerath et al. 2018) within visual space. The visual perceptions are stimulated by motion and dynamics and oscillatory activities. These factors drive the brain activity for visual processing, decomposing information, and analyzing the effects of visual consciousness.

E-commerce platforms displaying fashion apparel can be successful with user-friendly technology by optimizing the information at a single click. Virtual retailers of fashion products need to understand the shoppers' perspective for personalizing 3D store atmospherics (Ha et al. 2007). Though consumers enjoy browsing products, they might lose interest if navigation becomes complex and non-suggestive to explore identical or similar products. Firms engaged in the marketing of fashion apparel through virtual platforms need to ensure the display of varieties and arraying of products facilitate easy search with no time limits for making buying decisions. Hurrying consumers to make buying decisions and time-bound canceling of shopping carts not only cause dissatisfaction but also build distrust toward the brand. Product attractiveness should be the primary concern for retailers to build their virtual stores, which also matters to consumers in navigating the products. The navigational support can be enhanced by displaying suggestive products with visual endorsements (videos) to develop awareness, comprehension, conviction, and action among consumers engaged in virtual shopping. The anthropomorphic emotions can be developed by retailers through celebrity endorsements, consumer-oriented videos, and social voices. Virtual retailers should consider modularization of displaying, arraying, and recommending contextual products by similar design, color, size, fashion trends, seasonality, and perceived use values. The anthropomorphic emotions contribute to self-actualization and self-esteem, which helps consumers in non-conflictive decision-making. Virtual retailers should also develop online simulators based on anthropometric data of consumers to drive visual stimulus and help them in experiencing the body image congruence with apparels. Online fashion apparel retailing firms should also be engaged in developing user-generated content through communications on social media encouraging experiential videos, slogans, and reviews. In addition, retailing firms also need to conduct data-text mining to learn about consumer experiences posted on discrete platforms like micro-blogs (Rajagopal and Rajagopal 2023).

Machine Power and Proximity

Artificial intelligence (AI) in marketing has a new space to grow in customer-centric firms. AI has gone beyond robotics structures for customers, as it is now emerging as a tool for decision-making among consumer-oriented firms. Coding multiple information and communication technologies (ICT) has been central to value creation and has provided efficient services for enhancing consumers' experiences. AI is now able to manage data analysis and deliver managerial decisions to tourism firms. However, the human element is not totally replaced with machines in managing firms. AI is integrated with ICTs to be omnipresent in all stages of a tourist's journey and supports the ecstasy of customers (Buhalis et al. 2019). Early in this century, social robots played a pivotal role in serving the social institutions and tourism industry to disseminate information and converse with humans. Broadly, Alexa and Siri are also accommodated as social robots with AI to interact with humans. The ChatGPT has the new AI revolution in the public domain to develop interactive relationship and mutual dependency to learn and widen the information silos. AI robots serve as coworkers and analysts for decision-making in large multi-brand and international customer-centric firms. AI has yet to support tourism and hospitality industry robots with trust, anticipation, and emotions. Happiness, arousal, and merriment have a significant impact on robot sentiment polarity, while anticipation and surprise do not significantly affect the AI logarithms. Therefore, one major challenge is to anthropomorphize robots for tourism and hospitality industry (Jörling et al. 2019).

Coevolving with consumers and stakeholders, firms can identify appropriate technologies, carry out innovations, and prepare for effective technology transfer through training programs on face-to-face and digital platforms. Such integrated efforts leverage social and industrial consciousness for developing new products in the fields of renewable energy and sustainability and meeting social challenges like poverty alleviation, housing, and community health. The technological revolution has driven the digital transformation, as firms are engaged in cocreating value in industrial markets. Among the many forms of technology development, digital technologies have encouraged artificial intelligence, which has the strongest pervasive impact (Molina and Rajagopal 2023). Corporate giants like Amazon and FedEx have already been experimenting with sending delivery robots to doorsteps. Now, Piaggio, the Italian company that makes the Vespa scooter, is offering a stylish alternative (brand name GITA) of utilitarian machines, which could carry a weight up to 50 pounds (lbs.) and stroll along with the shoppers within the market space. There are two attractions associated with this AI robot to drive proximity: social attraction to the product and opening hedonic conversation for a utilitarian product. The AI is being actively used in public parks to regulate resource use and reinforce the basic civil laws in public places. Robot dog, a machine with AI and cameras, is used for surveillance and maintaining social distancing during the Covid-19 pandemic (2020–2022) in Singapore. In a real-life situation, using AI to train dogs and train low-cost robots to perform tasks previously achievable by machines is 10 times more expensive (Hsu 2022).

ICT and AI make a strong contribution to adventure shopping. American retailers that excel at adventure shopping manifestation fetch the highest sales per square foot in leisure and sport streams. Customers seem to happily wait in the long queues and chaos to experience the adventure shopping in stores, where the merchandise is ever-changing and unpredictable, prices are usually acceptable, and goods are of high quality. Macy's for apparel and housewares, TJ Maxx in varied merchandise, and Costco for innovative products along with utilitarian items can be good examples of adventure shopping in the United States. It is all about spotting surprises, taking a trial, and sharing experiences on digital media within known and unknown communities. Such customer interactions lead to generate 360° proximity and relationship.

Eudaimonism in proximity relationships is an attractive attribute of tourists to gain a sense of self-achievement, ultimately leading to health and well-being. The ICT and AI complement tourist knowledge, help in narrowing down the unveiled biases, and encourage eudaimonic behavior in adventure tourism. Adventure shopping enhances eudaimonic emotions, which are marginally different from perceived happiness or hedonic pleasure (George et al. 2021). However, when proximity products and services are commoditized, their benefits would enormously serve customer-centric firms. AI-based robots, unlike machines with predefined functions, could revolutionize retail industry by offering interactive solutions. Cutting-edge technologies significantly affect social and industrial development in transitional economies. The prominent technological edges that drive challenge-based research include artificial intelligence, AR, VR, wearable technology, robotics, and Big Data analytics. Growing environmental concerns, public policies, and scientific communities describe the efforts that utilize ecosystem processes to boost challenge-based research in engineering and technology to address societal challenges. The challenge-based research outputs have significantly contributed to the development of the consumer sector economy.

The technological revolution has driven the digital transformation, as firms are engaged in cocreating value to improve the markets in the services sector by adding the power of AI to acquire new customers. Among the many forms of technology development, digital technologies have encouraged AI, which has the strongest pervasive impact. By mobilizing resources and capitalizing on the growing AI revolution, firms in tourism and hospitality industry can converge this sector with the mainstream technology revolution of Industry 4.0. However, knowledge and skills, service design process, and cocreation of BMs in core services industry must be congruent with the embedded PNS factors in the society (Leone et al. 2021). Social relations widely rely on information technology infrastructure, irrespective of its sophistication. The major concern in digitalizing emotions and social relationships is to ensure effective knowledge management through diffusion of dialogues across social genres. Social empowerment depends on active digital connectivity in which people exchange their perceptions and values on brands, benefits, and benevolence (3Bs) to express their compassion to companies within the existing social ecology. Convergence of business and social ecology drives expectations of consumers and stakeholders to strengthen their association and social fit with both insiders and outsiders of their social regime. Such sociological bonding with business allows for sharing and mobilizing knowledge to identify opportunities of social well-being and reconstructing effective and efficient relationship channels to integrate changing business philosophies (Gupta and Govindarajan 2000).

Virtual Engagement

Enormous growth in information technology has shifted the social practice of face-to-face interactions to digital discussion platforms. Such a shift has widened the outreach of customers and increased the inflow of participants' information. Consequently, social media has become a major tool for crowdsourcing and managing data related to collective intelligence. The digital platforms for sharing personal opinions, new ideas, and experiences have transformed the conventional wisdom of people to stick to the brick-and-mortar forums, organize community meetings, and share experiences. Yet, community cultural centers serve in different sectors like social health, natural medicinal forums, handicrafts, and handloom cooperative center as the places of human relations in developing countries. Social networks are also supported by self-help groups working on specific social and economic themes like women empowerment, women entrepreneurship, sustainability, and many more. Similarly, social rights activists, business leaders, and political groups also promote communication hubs that attract participants to share their experience and new ideas related to the development of society and economy. Social relations widely rely on information technology infrastructure, irrespective of its sophistication. The major concern in digitalizing emotions and social relationships is to ensure effective knowledge management through diffusion of dialogues across the social genre. Social empowerment depends on active digital connectivity in which people exchange their perceptions and values on brands, benefits, and benevolence (3Bs) to express their compassion to companies within existing social ecology. Convergence of business and social ecology drives expectations of consumers and stakeholders to strengthen their association and social fit with both insiders and outsiders of their social regime. Such sociological bonding with business allows for sharing and mobilizing knowledge to identify opportunities for social well-being and reconstructing effective and efficient relationship channels to integrate changing business philosophies (Gupta and Govindarajan 2000).

The web-based relationship infrastructure has been enormously supported by stakeholders and supporters online for exchange of views about a business or a social cause. Consequently, collective intelligence has become a principal knowledge repository that fosters consumers' economic empowerment and a democratic transformation of the business sector in small and large enterprises. Though there are complexities in managing digital ethics in exchanging opinions on social media platforms, there is a need to set ethical norms via social and voluntary approaches to manage the social information dynamics on digital platforms rather than enforcing formal institutional mechanisms. The proximity of social institutions to business and innovation not only helps in building collective behavior of consumers but also encourages utilitarian and low-cost innovations through startup enterprises. The proximity of social interactive groups inculcates consciousness on consumption and sustainability through social engagement, empowerment, and public participation embodying crowdsourced and crowdfunded entrepreneurial and corporate activities. Consequently, proximity marketing plays a vital role in promoting consumer consciousness, innovation, and social marketing prospects with low cost and encourages effective operations in the niche market (Sedalo et al. 2022). The combination of proximity marketing, socialization of business, and hybridity has significantly encouraged the prospects of social marketing to promote a democratic philosophy in marketing strategies of large multinational companies. Such a shift in the B-to-C, C-to-C, and O-to-O marketing strategies has driven new relationships between consumers, markets, and companies. Social elements such as leader–member exchange (LMX) and information management through collective intelligence help customer-centric companies in developing proximity marketing model focusing not only on achieving customer outreach through empowerment of vulnerable segments like women and low-resource entrepreneurs but also on generating value by socializing the business. The social capital generation can be linked to social networks, and enhancing customer outreach, while triggering crowd behavior in support of brands and corporate images. Effective social governance of marketing communication and shared narratives targeting social factors help in attracting crowds.

The free flow of information is essential to well-functioning democracies and consumer marketplaces since both politicians and marketers need a communication system that has long outreach. It is not always simple—there are privacy issues, government regulations, and lack of access for many people. However, many see the democratization of information as offering possibilities for new forms of citizen engagement and empowerment that will give the people a greater voice in government and markets (Quelch and Jocz 2007). Consumer education must empower consumers through developing skills to enable them to make appropriate decisions. This is not enough in a rapidly changing world where consumers face completely new challenges (Jarva 2011). Consumer empowerment is a psychological construct related to the individual's perception of the extent to which they can control the distribution and use of their personally identifying information. It has been argued to have an impact on consumers' privacy concerns and trust in e-commerce. However, very little is known about the difference in male and female perceptions of this control. This investigation is focused on examining how perceptions concerning consumer empowerment and privacy concerns differ between the genders and how consumer empowerment results in perceptions of trust and decrease in privacy concerns (Midha 2012).

The role of marketing strategies in fostering controlled consumer empowerment is reflected in the development of information-based, consumer-centric marketing strategies that seek to enable, control, monitor, and promote proximity of firms within the society. In designing such strategies, consumers' familiarity with the use of ICTs is both strengthened and widened, emphasizing the uncontrolled nature of consumer empowerment process. There is a need to regain control over the marketing process, that is, to either manage the technological empowerment of consumers, or to devise new strategies cognizant of the possibility that such technological empowerment cannot be managed. The valuation of consumer loyalty in this environment rises significantly (Pires et al. 2006). The social domain intends to promote sustainability-led businesses and drive bottom-up (local) economy. The public domain drives social innovation through collective intelligence (crowdsourcing) for ideation and contextual information pooling, and crowdfunding to cocreate and coevolve crowd-based BMs.

Social empowerment of consumers has been adopted by many companies as a tool to build trust on the companies and their market ecosystem. Consumer-centric companies like LEGO (Denmark), IKEA (Sweden), Mary Kay Cosmetics (United States), and AMUL (India) have gained prominence in business by socially empowering their consumers and engaging them in the cocreation process. Social empowerment of consumers and their emotional stakes in designing new products and marketing is largely founded on the mutual trust between the consumers and the company. In this context, trust, as a driver of social empowerment, can be defined as the willingness to be open and adaptable to business policy and exhibit cooperative behavior through mutual belief in a consistent and predictable manner (Gefen 2000). Value perceptions among customers are induced by social, economic, and relational factors. The social learning theory explains this phenomenon as positive reinforcement, which occurs when a behavior (response) is followed by a favorable stimulus (commonly seen as pleasant) that increases the frequency of that behavior. In the conceptual foundations of social learning theory, respondent conditioning and observational learning are empirically supported approaches to understand normative human development and the etiology of psychosocial problems. The social learning process is widely influenced by the manifold growth of social media, digital networks, and interpersonal communications. Information technology has dramatically changed the social communication inflow by customers sharing their experiences, values, new product ideas, and complaints about companies and products. Online customer reviews extend word-of-mouth from new acquaintances and transform information from personal to public channels on social media platforms where interactions among experienced customers occur (Pfeffer et al. 2014).

Web-Design Blueprint for E-commerce

A well-designed e-commerce website supports in increasing sales, building confidence with customers, and ultimately driving business growth with competitiveness. However, designing effective e-commerce website requires eye-catching layout, embedded technology (3D product vision), shopping cart, user-friendly payment process, and customer services with self-service and reverse logistics facilities. Creating a blueprint for an e-commerce website involves several key steps to ensure a smooth and effective user experience. The stepwise blueprint of e-commerce web design is discussed as below:

Preparation for E-commerce Website Design

Market research is essential for e-commerce firms to understand existing market competition and consumer profile. Competitor analysis focuses on understanding the underlying strengths and weaknesses of competing firms. Consumer preferences and behavior need to be researched, and critical indicators should be used to exhibit the information on the website. Accordingly, the competitive and consumer insights will help firms to collect appropriate and adequate information for the website. Clear content on the profile of the firm describing the genesis, vision, mission, and goals of the firms along with its business philosophy attracts consumers to navigate the website and gain brand awareness. Site structure and navigation path can be developed by designing the following pages:

- Homepage: Clear and engaging with easy navigation along the contents about the firm, chronological growth, business philosophy, vision, mission, and goals of the firm. The inclusion of sustainability program and customer values on this page will provide an added advantage for consumers to learn about the firm from a competitive perspective. Placing text, images, dashboards, and interactive videos on the home page will generate awareness and interest and promote consumer engagement with the firm while navigating the page.
- Product Pages: Detailed descriptions of products by categories, arrays of products by categories, high-quality images, and customer

reviews constitute the core of product pages. These webpages must be developed with focus on product features, design and colors variations, adaptability or using process, holistic perspectives, 3D images or rotation of products, music, branding descriptions, and user reviews. Consistent use of colors, fonts, and logos will add value to build consumers' interest and stimulate buying intention. Responsive design of product pages must be ensured about the functionality of all product pages and embedded product features to help consumers to navigate the site on all devices. Product pages are based on the logical grouping of products for easy browsing with efficient search bar and filters.

- User Interface (UI): User interface of an e-commerce website plays a crucial role in providing a seamless and enjoyable shopping experience, which requires an intuitive and user-friendly layout. Simple and clear navigation menus to help users find products easily and implementing the breadcrumbs to show users their location within the site help smooth user navigation that allows for easy backtracking of contents and pages. Strategically placed clear and visible call-to-action functions like "Add to Cart" and "Buy Now" enable consumers to take advantage of easy buying solutions and the click-and-buy experience. Optimizing images on product pages is one of the major challenges for e-commerce firms, particularly with providing high UI and ensuring quick loading times of scripts. To gain customer confidence, it is necessary to value customers' opinion and display customer reviews and ratings prominently on product pages. E-commerce firms must offer easy ways for users to give feedback on their shopping experience.

Homepage is the face of the business. Therefore, chronological business performance including the expected performance of the firm in the current financial year with key performance indicators like investment, sales analytics, customer acquisition, market share, and customer ratings can be exhibited on the homepage to reinforce the organizational image. However, it is necessary to strategically manage the cost centers, market share, competitive promotions, and profitability of the firm. Though the market for e-commerce is boundary-less, a predetermined operational area by defining geographic access for ordering, deliveries, and offering services improves the efficiency of virtual business. Accordingly, planning organizational structure by regions and product-mix along with the business alliances to expand regional e-commerce proximity can be facilitated by the firms. In addition, it is necessary for the firms to identify the needs and preferences of target audience by understanding the PNS factors comprising problems, needs, and solutions. In a competitive hybrid retail business environment, consumers today buy solutions that satisfy their problems than merely products. Consequently, creating an intuitive interface solves their problems and builds effective relations between the firm and consumers.

Resource Planning

Planning human, capital, and technology recourses in virtual business firms is essential for ensuring efficient operations and achieving strategic goals. It is important for firms to identify strategic initiatives by aligning financial resources with the company's strategic goals, which can be used for market expansion, customer acquisition, product development, and innovation to stay competitive in the market. Accordingly, virtual business firms in B-to-C, B-to-B or hybrid segments plan to focus on high-impact projects that drive business growth. It is necessary for the firms to identify available resources including personnel, tools, and budget for strategic expansions, market research, and innovation and technology upgrades to plan and implement strategic and competitive business decisions. Simultaneously, firms also need to consider limitations such as budget caps, skill shortages, and time constraints to implement effective resources utilization. Alongside the management of financial resources, it is also important for the e-commerce businesses to hire skilled talents and manage team-based human resources suitable to the requirements of business projects. Technology tools like Asana, Trello, or Microsoft Teams can be used by firms to manage project tasks and track progress, while communication platforms like Zoom or social media channels can be used to coordinate across geographically distant teams. By following these strategies, virtual business firms can optimize their resource-planning processes, ensuring that they are well-equipped to meet their strategic objectives and adapt to changing circumstances.

E-commerce Technology

E-commerce technology encompasses a wide range of tools and platforms that enable online businesses to operate efficiently and provide a seamless shopping experience. Chatbots and intelligent virtual assistants improve functionality of e-commerce platforms. Consequently, these tools are commonly embedded in the B-to-C and B-to-B e-commerce platforms. These tools use natural language processing and machine learning to handle customer inquiries in real-time, providing personalized shopping experiences and improved customer service. Instant messaging, SMS, and electronic mail functions also help businesses to customize design, automate, and deliver personalized messages and promotional campaigns to engage customers and drive sales in a competitive market environment. Broadly, the impact of technology in improving the functionality and overall business efficiency can be seen in the following manner:

- Improving the functionality of website platform in order processing, interactive ordering, AI integration as customer support tool, 2D and 3D images, product videos, and user-generated verbal content.
- Exhibiting product information by displaying product attributes through verbal and nonverbal content, applications to demonstrate product functionality, customer reviews supported by data-text mining, and user-generated content.
- Integrating process integration using lean six-sigma methodology to process and monitor customer orders; storage of client information on cloud and conducting data analytics; setting delivery options, tracking through radio frequency identification (RFID) technology; and analyzing continuous customer feedback.
- Managing reverse logistics through relocations of deliveries and returns and handling alternate shipments using RFID, QR, satellite tracking, and mobile applications.

Image search engines like Google Images help customers to search for products using images, enhancing the online shopping experience by making it easier to find items. Over 60 percent of e-commerce sales are conducted on mobile applications as they provide a convenient platform for customers to shop, offering features like easy checkout and continuous brand interaction. Consequently, technology for m-commerce is highly advanced with significant impact on consumer buying. The technology platforms associated with e-commerce use machine learning to analyze customer behavior and suggest products, enhancing personalization and increasing sales, market share, and profitability of virtual businesses. The advance of technology use in marketing has integrated e-commerce processes within social media platforms, allowing users to discover and purchase products directly from social media applications. In addition, virtual reality (VR) creates immersive shopping experiences allowing customers to virtually try out products before purchasing. Technology solutions like sustainable packaging and distribution also aim to reduce the environmental impact of e-commerce operations through eco-friendly practices.

Virtual Store Organization

Organizing a virtual e-commerce store involves defining target customers, choosing a potential niche, selecting an e-commerce platform, designing a user-friendly website, setting up product listings with detailed descriptions, integrating payment processing, configuring shipping options, managing inventory, optimizing for search engines, and implementing marketing strategies to attract customers and drive sales. Virtual stores can be organized in the following manner:

- Product departments
- Product-mix (product categories, product line, and brands)
- Stock-keeping units and suppliers
- Structure of sales (own warehouse, third-party distribution)
- Sales promotions for store- and third-party brands

In e-commerce, the taxonomy of developing virtual store ergonomics is a major challenge. Virtual stores integrate different product departments, product line by categories, promotion content including verbal and nonverbal elements, recommended products, consumer reviews, and product demonstrations. The ergonomics of virtual stores designed with high-quality graphics by embedding the use of high-resolution images and smooth animations not only help consumers to navigate product pages of the virtual stores but also help in reducing visual strain. Attractive store ergonomics with lighting and colors schemes enhance product visibility and stimulate purchase intention among consumers. Virtual stores must ensure that interactions such as selecting and rotating products are embedded on the platform to encourage responsive and intuitive navigation. These stores should integrate feedback mechanisms to collect, exhibit, and analyze immediate feedback for user actions to confirm selections and actions.

Packaging and Delivery

One of the crucial aspects of e-commerce is packaging and delivery, which significantly impacts customer satisfaction and brand perception. The primary role of packaging is to protect the product during transit. Using materials like corrugated boxes, bubble wrap, and packing peanuts ensures items reach undamaged at the destination. However, e-commerce firms must also assess the cost, time, and risk (CTR) factors associated with the packaging of products and maintain anonymity of brand for safe delivery of products. Offering multiple shipping options and breaking down the cost and estimated time of delivery such as standard, expedited, and same-day delivery will help customers customize their delivery and track shipments accordingly. Fulfillment centers of e-commerce firms enable streamlined delivery process and handle storage, packing, and shipping activities. Broad packaging designs include minimalist packaging, modular design, and reusable packing. The minimalist packing aims at reducing the amount of material used in packaging to significantly lower environmental impact while reusable packaging complies with sustainability goals. However, biodegradable packaging made with the materials like compostable paper and cardboards and biopolymers that can be broken down by microorganisms—such as bacteria, fungi, and algae—that return to their natural state comply with sustainable packaging.

Payment Planning

Easy and secured payment processing is one of the major challenges in e-commerce. It is a strategic process of selecting and integrating various payment methods on an online store, ensuring a smooth checkout experience for customers while considering sensitive factors like security, transaction fees, and customer preferences. Often e-commerce firms are associated with third-party payment gateways like Stripe, PayPal, or Square to process payments effectively by accepting different credit cards or debit cards. In addition, large e-commerce firms like Alibaba and Amazon have introduced their own payment wallets like Alipay and Amazon Pay, respectively. E-commerce firms must implement security measures to protect vital financial and personal data of consumers against fraudulent transactions, including address verification, CVV codes, and monitoring suspicious activity.

Data Security

Protecting vital information of consumers related to payment instrument and devices is a critical aspect of e-commerce, which demands continuous surveillance from cyberthreats. Secure Sockets Layer (SSL) certificates encrypt data and prevent unauthorized access to information transmitted between users, banks, and the firm's servers, which will protect sensitive information of consumer orders, credit card details, and bank details; in addition, using firewalls help block unauthorized access and use of anti-malware software helps detect and remove malicious software. Networking with reputable payment gateways that complies with the Payment Card Industry Data Security Standard (PCI-DSS) ensures secure transactions. The core areas of data security concerns are as follows:

- Client information encryption
- Server allocations and controls
- Transaction data
- Business partners' information
- Payment information

Implementing multifactor authentication for both customers and administrative access adds an additional layer of security in e-commerce transactions.

E-commerce websites should be hosted with the service provider that offers robust security features, including DDoS (Distributed Denial of Service) protection, regular backups, and malware scanning. DDoS protection refers to the measures taken to defend a network, application, or server from a DDoS attack, which aims to overpower a system with malicious traffic, rendering it unavailable to legitimate users by flooding it with requests from multiple sources. Accordingly, it is a system-designed program to detect and filter out malicious traffic while allowing legitimate access to continue functioning normally. Consumer education about phishing scams would add to increase the level of confidence among consumers and encourage them to use strong and unique passwords. E-commerce firms should develop compliance with relevant data protection regulations, such as Consumer Privacy Protection Acts of California and Utah, and Data Privacy Acts of Connecticut and Virginia in the United States.

Reviews and Actions

In the e-commerce industry, feedback provided by customers about their experiences with a product or service is very significant to understand the perceived values, satisfaction, and their behavioral inclination to recommend the e-commerce website to peers. Consumer opinion is typically displayed by the firms on a website or marketplace, while client actions encompass the specific steps a customer takes on an e-commerce platform, such as browsing products, adding items to a cart, making a purchase, or leaving a negative review on the website of the firm or on third-party Internet blogs or social media channels. The key client actions in e-commerce are listed as follows:

- Browsing: Navigating through product categories and listings on a website.
- Adding to cart: Selecting products and placing them in a virtual shopping cart.
- Checkout: Completing the purchase process by providing shipping and payment information.
- Returning items: Initiating a return process for a purchased product.

- Writing reviews: Sharing feedback about a product or service on the website or a review platform.
- Wish listing: Saving products for future consideration.
- Engaging with social media: Interacting with a brand's social media posts about products.

It is very important for firms to respond to the reviews of consumers. Monitoring consumer behavior and using analytics tools to understand customer actions on the website help e-commerce firms to be competitive, customer-centric, and updated with consumer preferences. Periodic analysis of customer reviews will also help firms to identify potential underlying issues and develop pro-customer approaches to enhance e-commerce business. Customer feedback includes the following actions:

- Opinions, testimonials, and referrals
- Satisfaction rating
- Corporate response and client review conformity
- Complaint handling and solutions

Positive reviews act as social endorsement, building trust with potential customers and encouraging them stay loyal to stimulate other consumers to develop purchase intentions. Customers often rely on reviews to make buying decision, especially when caught in dilemma. Positive reviews significantly impact a website's search engine ranking, while negative reviews provide valuable insight into areas where a business can be improved to gain competitive advantage.

Reverse Logistics

Reverse logistics is the process of managing the goods returned by buyers to their original location. This is a post-delivery stage of supply chain and logistics. In e-commerce, the return of goods is common due to mismatch between ordered products and delivered products or damage in transit. However, often consumers express quality concerns while returning the products back to the e-commerce company or third-party suppliers. Handling customer returns includes processing of returns quickly, visibly, and controllably by allowing customer to self-generate reverse logistics QR code from the e-commerce website of the firm and routing the shipment through pre-contracted logistics service provider. Upon return, products need to be inspected to determine where they should be placed next in the process. Once a product is returned, it should be thoroughly screened for damage and subjected to refurbishment, recycling, or repacked for resale to fill another order. If the products belong to third-part suppliers, usually they are returned to them by e-commerce firms. E-commerce firms like Amazon and Alibaba have streamlined their reverse-logistics processes to manage returned goods before it arrives.

Marketing Planning

The development of marketing plans has been the cornerstone of marketing firms, which is instilled as a ritual among generations of e-commerce and brick-and-mortar retail firms. Creating a marketing plan involves several key stages to ensure a comprehensive and effective strategy. These stages broadly involve specific, measurable, achievable, relevant, and time-bound (SMART) goals to guide the marketing planning process. The key stages in marketing planning process are listed below:

- Determine the size of the company by estimating the volume of orders, sales, and customer traffic,
- Develop customer acquisition and retention strategies by generating loyalty or cross-selling promotions,
- Implement marketing-mix strategies and measure its effectiveness,
- Develop effective digital advertisements and embed them on the product webpages and link product sales with crowd-based campaigns on social media channels,
- Plan expansion of business through vertical (specialization) and horizontal (generalization) strategies,
- Exhibit differentiation and diversification on products, promotions, and processes through visual merchandising by equipping product pages with appropriate verbal- and nonverbal information,

- Employ advertising revenue model such as direct, pay-per-click, or institutional approaches, and
- It is also important to ensure service integration to gain customer satisfaction and functional effectiveness.

An effective marketing plan can help a business grow and increase its revenue by capitalizing on market opportunities. Marketing planning capability involves strategic marketing decisions, selection of market segments, corporate objectives, value proposition, and timing for a wide range of planned e-commerce activities. Nonetheless, marketing planning needs a total digital transformation from a conventional practice to operate in real-time, reflect continuous changes, and account for new information and opportunities in the competitive marketplace as they arise.

Case Studies

CS1: *Babyonline E-commerce*

Suzhou Beibao E-Commerce Co. Ltd, also known as *Babyonline*, is a company based in Suzhou, China. Established in 2012, Babyonline specializes in cross-border e-commerce, particularly in the wedding dress industry. The company has leveraged its expertise in product sourcing, quality control, and online platform management to build a strong brand reputation. Babyonline had moved to a make-to-stock system in 2015, which lowered costs but seemed to have raised inventory issues. In the changing market trends, selective selling by some sales representatives had led to structural inventory problems. Over time, around 2018, the wedding dress industry in Suzhou, China, was confronted with severe low demand causing business shutdown, which required all unqualified wedding dress factories to move out of the market within 1 week.

Babyonline emerged as a cross-broader e-commerce company focusing on selling wedding dresses internationally, navigating the complexities of cross-border logistics and payment processing. The company initially adopted a *make-to-stock* business model to lower costs, but this led to inventory issues that required strategic adjustments. A make-to-stock business model refers to a production strategy where a company manufactures goods in advance based on anticipated customer demand, essentially stocking finished products in inventory ready for immediate sale rather than waiting for individual customer orders to place production runs. This strategy not only allows for faster delivery times but can also lead to risks of overstocking and potential obsolescence if demand forecasts are inaccurate. Babyonline estimated future demand and produced wedding dresses in bulk according to that prediction, which went into slump in an interval of 3 years. However, the company found that maintaining appropriate stock levels might jeopardize sales, as consumer preferences might change unnoticed even though enough products were available without incurring high carrying costs due to excess inventory. This business model faced difficulty in quickly responding to sudden changes in demand due to radical shifts in customer preferences. However, the company has explored various strategies such as strategic alliances, market development, and product diversification, to sustain growth and competitive advantage to overcome the embedded risks of make-to-stock business model.

The strength of the Babyonline business model is that it enjoys a highly competitive brand reputation in China with specialization in product sourcing and quality control. Robust online platform, logistics infrastructure, and data-driven marketing and customer segmentation strategies of the company focus on customer service and positive customer reviews of the make-to-stock approach of bridal dresses in China. However, the brand had lower international recognition, as company had less experience in navigating foreign regulations and cultural nuances to meet potential challenges toward logistical operations, aligning prices with currency fluctuations, and dealing with the payment-processing complexities.

Over time, Babyonline had faced competition from established international players, and crossing the trade barriers and regulatory changes was one of the major challenges for the company, besides sailing through fluctuating exchange rates, economic uncertainties, cybersecurity risks, and data privacy concerns. However, in some parts of Southeast Asia and Europe, the demand for high-quality baby products has been increasing since the mid-2020s, which had opened partnerships with international brands and retailers. The company narrowed down its scope of business during the post-pandemic period by focusing on customized product offerings and sharing promotions through messages on social media channels and extended customer service to the specific needs and preferences of target customers.

CS2: *Marketing Technology of Nike Shoes*

Nike, Inc. is an American athletic footwear and apparel corporation at Beaverton, Oregon, United States as its headquarters. The company uses virtual reality (VR)–based design software and simulation tools to collaborate in real-time between designers, engineers, and developers. This technological intervention enables the company with faster designing and testing of prototypes. This reduces the need for physical product samples and manual quality checks. The Athlete-Imagined Revolution (AIR) collection of shoes feature 3D-printed sneakers designed by athletes and brought to life by Nike's innovative designs. In all, NIKE worked with 13 athletes and dedicated the artificially intelligence (AI) designed sneakers across four different sports—comprising track (running), global football, basketball, and tennis. The 13 prototypes of AIR sneakers manufactured with blazing colors and semi-translucent and hardened 3D-printed material glow under the seemingly UV light making the hot-orange color-way look like fired glass. Consequently, Nike's AIR initiative leverages AI to cocreate shoe designs with athletes. This process involves generating hundreds of design concepts quickly, which are then refined based on athletes' input.

Nike's Fit Application includes a feature called Nike Fit that uses augmented reality (AR) to measure a customer's feet and recommend the right shoe size. The company also uses augmented reality (AR) to blur the lines between real and virtual life. Customers can use AR to plan the home décor and ergonomics in rooms to suit their lifestyle and emotions. The development of Nike Air Max Scorpion shoe model involved 3D, VR design software, computational design, and engineering tools in addition to the machine learning and digital-twin technologies.

The concept of a metaverse, which is a fully immersive and interconnected virtual world, is becoming increasingly popular with the technology. Metaverse is an attractive place for brands to connect with their customers using innovative marketing techniques. Nike Metaverse has been established with *Swoosh* Web3-enabled portal as a hub for its non-fungible tokens (NFTs) and virtual collectibles. With their prior success with Nikeland, it is not surprising that Nike is diving deeper into the virtual collectible market. Using NFTs enables the company to build a community by engaging users in the digital realm with collectible objects. Nike's patent of 2019 protects the technology needed to collect, trade, and sell digital accessories or wearables as NFTs. Nike collaborated with RTFKT, a company that creates digital artifacts, including sneakers and collectibles, to create real-life *Cryptokicks* that feature an automatically adjusting lacing system (Design Booms, n.d.). Nike's Cryptokicks are a collection of customizable sneakers using non-fungible token (NFT) and combine both digital and physical worlds.

Nike uses 3D printing for rapid prototyping and creating custom shoes for elite athletes. This technology allows for precise adjustments based on athlete feedback and can significantly speed up the design process. Designers of Nike use software like Adobe Illustrator, Corel Draw, and 3D-modeling programs to create detailed models of the shoes before they are prototyped. These technologies help Nike stay at the forefront of innovation in the footwear industry, ensuring that their products meet the highest standards of performance and comfort expected by athletes and consumers alike.

Summary

Various aspects of e-commerce architecture include technology infrastructure and visualization aspects that have been central to the discussion in this chapter. Architecting an e-commerce firm is a challenging task and need to comply with various requirements related to technology infrastructure to enable high-speed display of website content and navigation besides identifying target audience, analyzing existing market competition, setting up clear goals, choosing right suppliers, and appropriate marketing channels. It is argued in the chapter that fundamentally e-commerce is all about creating user-efficient buying platforms and virtual store displays along with setting up order processing and delivery management. It is important for firms to optimize e-commerce website for search engines through the search engine optimization (SEO) process. The requirement for the right webservers to support the inflow and outflow of products, processes, and services needs evaluating both current and future resource requirements, traffic projections, and budgeting. The chapter deliberates on creating the visualization impact in e-commerce and suggests that every product in a category should have a homepage, which helps showcase new products, bestsellers, and promotions to grab attention. In addition, the product homepage must also showcase recommended products matching the attributes of products and consumer search intentions. Showcasing recommended products can be based on generative artificial intelligence (AI) and consumer navigation data analytics. In addition to customized visualization of products on e-commerce platforms, the discussion in this chapter proposes that firms must collect data of consumer choices about verbal and nonverbal content, use values, price, process, promotion, customer reviews, colors, images, videos, and the like.

It is important to learn that virtual merchandising blended with virtual store ergonomics, product dimensions, and sensory experience tends to instantly substitute the need for physical touch, feel, and pick emotions of customers and delivers the satisfaction virtually in e-commerce transactions. The chapter argues that machine power and visual effects on e-commerce platforms help firms in enhancing hybrid proximity (physical and virtual) among customers and encourage virtual engagement. The seamless ambience of virtual business technology has grown in the 21st century and has spread across IoT and Metaverse Reality (MR), going beyond AR and VR, as has been discussed in this chapter. The contemporary tools to develop techno-biz models in specific sectors such as consumer health and well-being, electronic home appliances, fashion, value, and lifestyle products have also been discussed. This chapter provides an e-commerce website development blueprint that guides new entrepreneurs in managing e-commerce business. Arguments and critical discussions in this chapter also include the long-term (strategic) versus short-term (tactical) impact of virtual marketing on the competitiveness and performance of customer-centric businesses. The above discussions are illustrated by the case study of Babyonline e-commerce company of China and the successful use of advanced marketing technology, including AI, VR, and metaverse, by Nike Inc. in promoting its technology-led shoes.

References

Buhalis, D., T. Harwood, V. Bogicevic, G. Viglia, S. Beldona, and C. Hofacker. 2019. "Technological Disruptions in Services: Lessons from Tourism and Hospitality." *Journal of Service Management* 30 (4): 484–506.

Design Booms. (n.d.). "NIKE Brings RTFKT's Sneaker NFTs to Life with 'Cryptokicks iRL' Series." Accessed November 29, 2024. https://www.designboom.com/design/nike-rtfkt-sneaker-nft-real-life-cryptokicks-irl-12-06-2022/.

Gefen, D. 2000. "e-Commerce: The Role of Familiarity and Trust." *Omega* 28 (6): 725–37.

George, A. J., E. Rajkumar, R. John, R. Lakshmi, and M. Wajid. 2021. "Mindfulness-Based Eudaimonic Enhancement for Well-Being of Individuals with Alcohol-Dependence: A Pilot Randomized Controlled Study." *Open Psychology Journal* 14 (1): 167–78.

Gupta, A., and V. Govindarajan. 2000. "Knowledge Management's Social Dimension: Lessons from Nucor Steel." *MIT Sloan Management Review* 42 (1): 71–81.

Ha, Y., W. Kwon, and S. J. Lennon. 2007. "Online Visual Merchandising (VMD) of Apparel Web Sites." *Journal of Fashion Marketing and Management* 11 (4): 477–93.

Hsu, J. 2022. "Using AI to Train Robot Dogs Makes Them Cheaper." *New Scientist* 256 (3411): 14.

Himel, E. 2023. "Choosing the Right Server for Your E-Commerce Business: A Comprehensive Guide. Bitbyte Technology Ltd." Accessed November 22, 2024. https://bitbytetechnology.com/blog/choosing-the-right-server-for-your-e-commerce-business-a-comprehensive-guide/.

Jarva, V. 2011. "Consumer Education and Everyday Futures Work." *Futures* 43 (1): 99–111.

Jerath, R., S. M. Cearley, V. A. Barnes, and M. Jensen. 2018. "Micro-Calibration of Space and Motion by Photoreceptors Synchronized in Parallel with Cortical Oscillations: A Unified Theory of Visual Perception." *Medical Hypotheses* 110: 71–5.

Jörling, M., R. Böhm, and S. Paluch. 2019. "Service Robots: Drivers Perceived Responsibility for Service Outcomes." *Journal of Service Research* 22 (4): 404–20.

Juntunen, M., E. Ismagilova, and E. L. Oikarinen. 2019. "B2B Brands on Twitter: Engaging Users with a Varying Combination of Social Media Content Objectives, Strategies, and Tactics." *Industrial Marketing Management* 89: 630–41.

Leone, D., F. Schiavone, F. P. Appio, and B. Chiao. 2021. "How Does Artificial Intelligence Enable and Enhance Value Co-Creation in Industrial Markets?

An Exploratory Case Study in the Healthcare Ecosystem." *Journal of Business Research* 129: 849–59.

Midha, V. 2012. "Impact of Consumer Empowerment on Online Trust: An Examination Across Genders." *Decision Support Systems* 54 (1): 198–205.

Molina, A., and Rajagopal. 2023. *Challenge-Based Learning, Research, and Innovation: Leveraging Industry, Government, and Society.* Cham, Switzerland: Springer (A Palgrave Macmillan Imprint).

Mostaghel, R., P. Oghazi, V. Parida, and V. Sohrabpour. 2022. "Digitalization Driven Retail Business Model Innovation: Evaluation of Past and Avenues for Future Research Trends." *Journal of Business Research* 146: 134–45.

Pfeffer, J., T. Zorbach, and K. M. Carley. 2014. "Understanding Online Firestorms: Negative Word-of-Mouth Dynamics in Social Media Networks." *Journal of Marketing Communications* 20 (1–2): 117–28.

Pires, G. D., J. Stanton, and P. Rita. 2006. "The Internet, Consumer Empowerment and Marketing Strategies." *European Journal of Marketing* 40 (9–10): 936–49.

Quelch, J. A., and K. A. Jocz. 2007, *Information: Knowledge Is Power—Leveraging Information in the Consumer and Political Marketplaces.* Boston, MA: Harvard Business School Press.

Rajagopal. 2024. *Proximity Marketing: Converging Community, Consciousness, and Consumption.* New York: Business Expert Press.

Rajagopal, and A. Rajagopal. 2023. "'Seeing Is Experiencing': Impact of Showcasing Fashion Merchandises on Digital Platforms." *Qualitative Market Research* 26 (3): 214–31.

Riegger, A. S., J. F. Klein, K. Merfeld, and S. Henkel. 2021. "Technology-Enabled Personalization in Retail Stores: Understanding Drivers and Barriers." *Journal of Business Research* 123: 140–55.

Sedalo, G., H. Boateng, and J. P. Kosiba. 2022. "Exploring Social Media Affordance in Relationship Marketing Practices in SMEs." *Digital Business* 2 (1): 100017. https://doi.org/10.1016/j.digbus.2021.100017.

Song, S. Y., and Y. K. Kim. 2020. "Factors Influencing Consumers' Intention to Adopt Fashion Robot Advisors: Psychological Network Analysis." *Clothing and Textiles Research Journal* 40 (1): 3–18.

Woo. (n.d.). "WooCommerce Server Recommendations." Accessed November 22, 2024. https://woocommerce.com/document/server-requirements/.

Zha, D., P. Foroudi, T. C. Melewar, and Z. Jin. 2022. "Experiencing the Sense of the Brand: The Mining, Processing and Application of Brand Data Through Sensory Brand Experiences." *Qualitative Market Research* 25 (2): 205–32.

CHAPTER 4

Behavioral Engagement

Overview

The customer-centric discussion domain of virtual market system with focus on consumer outreach, business expansion, and innovation and technology is central to this chapter. The chapter discusses holistic perspectives of behavioral engagement. This perspective focuses on online consumer behavior, virtual shopping patterns, and immersive experience in the virtual marketplace. The hybrid BMs integrating cyber–physical infrastructure meet the increasing challenges of the changing market ecosystem. The cyber–physical triadic marketing-design strategy comprising design-to-market, design-to-society, and design-to-value models (Rajagopal, 2021) as an innovative approach for the firms has also been discussed in this chapter. Besides the customer-centric, techno-economic, and socio-psychological perspectives of virtual marketing scenarios, managing SEO techniques and analyzing the transaction logs and supply chain trackers from manufacturing to delivery have been categorically addressed in this chapter. In addition, the chapter presents a discussion on the marketing value matrix, multichannel marketing, and T-3 elements comprising time, trust, and transparency that significantly affect the virtual marketing process.

The Techno-Social Shift

Continuous innovation and technology in consumer products companies have set new trends in the market and created dynamic value perceptions among consumers that have raised their preferences and expectations. Digital marketing has opened massive opportunities to deliver new consumer experiences and strengthened the relationships with consumers across destinations in the global marketplace. Digital disruption has created new dimensions in consumer marketing through benefits of large-scale promotions and convenience to drive compulsive buying behavior among consumers. The platform economy has shown a huge shift in the creation of consumer value. However, technology and born-digital businesses have led the innovations, which are being experienced by consumers in every sector now. The platform economy distinctly comprises a new set of business and economic relations that depend on the Internet, computation, and data. The ecosystem created by each platform is a source of value, and it sets the terms by which users can participate. Such businesses and economic platforms have empowered consumers and developed their bargaining potential for quality and value for money. Though digitalization in marketing has induced rapid shift in consumer behavior through open access to brand communication, consumer experiences, and sociopsychological cognition toward building their preferences and values, many multinationals are encouraging "value chain localization" strategies that still focus on only the premier segment of consumers. This strategy does not adequately prepare them to meet the greater challenge and opportunity of reaching out to remote consumers and achieving the universe of market by serving consumers of all segments including premier, mass (upper, regular, and lower stratum), and bottom-of-the-pyramid. Hindustan Unilever Limited (HUL), a consumer products company, has extensively reached the consumers at the bottom-of-the-pyramid to market its consumer brands by empowering rural women as sales representatives. HUL has created consumer behavior for its brands, upholding gender and societal values.

Most companies are inculcating radical buying behavior among consumers by generating brand literacy though the interactions of consumer communities on social media. Facebook, Twitter (now X), and Instagram are the principal platforms of consumer networking for most of the consumer-centric companies. Companies explore consumer needs and preferences on digital platforms and endeavor to meet consumers' rising expectations about the products and services they intend to buy. Simultaneously, to reaffirm their purchase intentions, consumers also stay critical to the multichannel experience of peers on their preferred brands. Consumer experience is diffused by user-generated content on social media, which illuminates their perceptions, attitude, and behavior toward a brand in the marketplace. For example, Nordstrom customers can buy products not only in the physical and virtual stores but also through a mobile app or on Instagram or via text message. Consumers can pick, return, or exchange their online purchases at Nordstrom stores. Such convenience of digital marketing to access reviews and referrals develops purchase intensions, and the possibility of decision reversals due to change in value perceptions has strengthened consumer attitude and behavior toward the brand.

In view of the above attributes of virtual consumer behavior, what matters the most is the way consumers make decisions to buy products online, including how they navigate over websites for the preferred items, analyzing vital product and marketing indicators across virtual stores and departments to make purchases. The behavioral alignment of consumer needs and product displays in stores refers to the psychological and cognitive processes involved in buying behavior. Among many factors that influence the consumer behavior in online shopping include the following socio-psychological attributes:

- Expectations: Consumers develop expectations about product availability, delivery, shipping costs, and the buying process. The expectation is built in the context of need, peer influence, and product attractiveness.
- Website design: The design of a website acts as a principal catalyst compelling consumers to navigate across different departments and products, which significantly impacts consumer behavior.
- Social media: Social media also influences consumer behavior through consumers' interactions with peers and the wider community justifying the needs, products, perceived use value, value for money, and associated promotions.
- Peer reviews: Consumers heavily rely on reviews from other customers to make decisions. Concerns of consumers on peer reviews are largely judgmental in the context of product value, price, promotions, and market trends.
- Trust: Consumers may be skeptical of online reviews, especially for health services. However, peer reviews as a collective emotion affect consumer cognition, trust, and loyalty.

- Credibility: The visual merchandising, array of consumer choices, and brand authenticity of the virtual shop impact consumer behavior.
- Payment security: The security of payment process affects consumers' intention to stay with the store. Protecting the privacy of vital personal information of consumers builds trust and impacts consumer behavior.

The COVID-19 pandemic period had highly encouraged consumers to shift toward virtual shopping and it reinforced consumer behavior after recovering businesses from the pandemic. One of the major attractions for the consumer to shop online is convenience. Consumers prioritize convenience to seek seamless experiences across devices and platforms. This includes easy navigation, quick checkouts, flexible payment options, and guaranteed reverse logistics. E-commerce firms encourage omnichannel marketing and shoppers expect a consistent experience through shopping online, on mobile apps, or in physical stores. Consequently, retailers need to integrate their online and offline channels effectively, which leads to hybrid business model. However, there has been significant decline in brand loyalty as consumers tend to switch brands based on availability, price, and convenience using the online shopping platforms. As prominent e-commerce firms like Amazon, Alibaba, and hybrid stores ensure fast and secured delivery of products purchased online, the speed and reliability of delivery remain crucial in influencing the consumer behavior. Consumers expect quick shipping and transparent tracking information.

Virtual Consumer Behavior

Shopping at virtual and brick-and-mortar stores is widely supported by the real use experiences, which are personified with the perceived value and extent of satisfaction by individual consumers. Systematic arraying of fashion accessories and apparel on virtual platforms demonstrates a cognitive illusion in a synthetic environment, which stimulates emotions virtual experience, and me-too-feeling among consumers. Watching products and analyzing their attributes provides multisensory experience and neurobehavioral stimuli to drive conscious consumption. An array of fashion accessories and apparel on virtual platforms with various portfolio pictures stimulates cognitive reasoning, semantics, and visualization of self-image to derive internal satisfaction and develop congruence with the products on virtually displayed fashion products. The virtual merchandising is the most evident virtual ergonomics, which proactively pushes experience-intensive customers to observe illusory experience on the products and develop purchase intentions (Rajagopal and Rajagopal 2023). Virtual shopping allows customers to browse products online as they would in a physical store. Such shopping facilities can include features like 3D product views, virtual try-ons, and interactive catalog. Shopper get personalized assistance as they can connect with online store associates using chat, video calls, or co-browsing sessions, which helps to enhance the in-store experience by gaining real-time assistance and personalized recommendations. Virtual shopping converges between online and offline channels by creating an omnichannel awareness about products and services and help in seeking seamless shopping experience. Consequently, customers start their shopping journey online and complete it in-store, or vice versa. Such consumer behavior has envisioned the *click-and-collect* or hybrid store model, which has been a success during the post-pandemic business recovery period. Online shopping behavior also enhances the consumer engagement with brands to create immersive experiences across the virtual showrooms, pop-up shops, and gamified shopping environments. A *click-and-collect* business model allow customers to purchase items online and then pick them up at a physical store location, essentially combining the convenience of online shopping with the ability to collect goods in person.

The experience-sharing over the digital platforms further influences the consumer behavior over a long time. Patterns of consumerism are changing in the society, as there are shifts in the consumer demography in the markets. The explosion of mass consumer segment, urbanization, and increase in the size of the population of aging consumers have contributed significantly to the shifts in consumer preferences and overall consumption behavior. Direct-to-customer (D-to-C) marketing strategies, convenience shopping, and social media-driven marketing approaches of companies have increased the social and cultural influence on developing the consumer behavior (Karagür et al., 2022). However, disruption in technology and attraction toward local consumption also contribute to driving consumer behavior dynamic across the geodemographic segments. Extended technology lifecycle builds positive consumer perceptions on higher value for money. Cocreation and codesigning approaches of customer-centric companies like IKEA has established business philosophy of connecting consumers and developing an emotion-based relationship with consumers as the key to leveraging loyalty and advocacy behavior.

Previous studies have defined the virtual experience in visualizing merchandise as a psychological state of feeling, which enhances merriment and arousal, visual enjoyment, perceptions related to self-image congruence and develops purchase intentions to transform the virtuality into real experience. The virtual merchandising on digital platforms drives self-endorsement and predetermined psychological effects induced by collective intelligence and hedonic disposition. The mainstream retailing industry has transformed from the traditional shopping practices to multichannel retailing by developing the retail business through e-commerce platforms. Such transformation in retailing technology has increased the global market outreach and online penetration of potential customers with increased visual satisfaction and ease-of-use of technology. The visualization features have allowed retailers to demonstrate the 3D store effect by allowing multiple presentations supported by visual technologies to provide sensory perceptions (Zha et al. 2022). The virtual merchandising blended with the virtual store ergonomics, product dimensions, and sensory experience tend to instantly substitute the need for physical inspection such as fitting, touching, and appearance satisfaction (Grewal et al. 2021). Effective merchandise display helps shoppers to coordinate a cross-product mix and develop purchase intentions. The visual merchandising stimulates self-image congruence, ontological reasoning, and neurobehavioral outcomes leading to perceptual stimuli and satisfaction reinforcing the feeling of *seeing is experiencing*. The positive attitude toward seeing, believing, and experiencing leads to a decision-making phenomenon within perceptual triangle of elements comprising knowing, experiencing, and being (Rajagopal and Rajagopal 2023).

Technology and Visual Merchandising

Visual merchandising is a marketing practice, which embodies both online and brick-and-mortar retailing practices and uses a variety of elements to attract customers and generate sales. These elements include virtual and physical store ergonomics including categorizing products by departments, arraying them on the product website, embedding augmented and VR technologies, floor plans, brightness, color, and audiovisual displays. Smart algorithms can group products together that are often purchased together, or suggest products based on a customer's search patterns. Shoppers can see details of textures and materials in greater clarity than with their own eyes. In the brick-and-mortar stores *ReStore for Retail* technology provides opportunity for managers and visual merchandisers to interact virtually on visual merchandising projects in real-time. Corporate managers can connect with each store location globally, allowing them to understand the look of their stores as their customers would experience it in the moment. Visual merchandisers can follow up and collating photos and reports from stores in relatively less time using the technology platforms, which proving them more time to review and coach store teams.

The virtual merchandising through clear arraying of product portfolios and simultaneous display of contextual products have given wide options to the consumers, which has supported buying decisions and enabled the business model innovation among the digital retail competitors). One of the major impacts of retail digital technologies has been toward 3V factors comprising value creation, value delivery, and value capture. The artificial intelligence (AI) and virtual reality (VR) have supported the consumer learning process on product design, attributes, and values, which have helped consumers to make appropriate buying decisions in a quick time (Capatina et al. 2020). In addition to AI and VR, the chatbots and robot-driven responses have enhanced the consumer experience online and supported consumer perceptions on *seeing is experiencing*. The fusion of brick-and-mortar shopping behavior with technology-led virtual shopping experiences have encouraged consumers to attain a holistic experience of virtual merchandising and an integrated buying experience. Virtual merchandising supported by enhanced products information, real-time prices, customization advise, order and delivery tracking, and information on purchased transactions have supported consumer perceptions and purchase intentions on various retail technology platforms (Riegger et al. 2021). The fashion apparel is effectively promoted on social media mainly targeting Twitter (now X), Facebook, Instagram, and

TikTok through emoticons, social speech tags, and unigrams and bigrams linguistic. The virtual display mannequins with anthropomorphic dimensions presenting the human-like musculoskeletal morphology attract consumers to explore the array of products on virtual retail sites to make instant purchase decisions. In addition, embedded videos of models anchoring vogue products on virtual retailing websites stimulate appearance similarity, physical congruence, and social consciousness among consumers to inculcate purchase intentions (Song and Kim 2020).

Visual stimuli develop cognitive reasoning and experience among consumers, which leads to perceived satisfaction and self-image congruence. Continuity in shopping across brands for seeking variety of fashion apparel, the consumer perceptions on the apparel designs and self-esteem significantly motivate the tacit and uniqueness needs of consumers. Such behavior driven by the product eye-tracking motivates purchase intentions and drives centrality of senses toward developing congruence with the product image and appearance perfectionism. The effect of arraying fashion apparel supported by dynamic postures significantly affects the women consumers and influence their personality traits, comparison of social appearances, and self-esteem. Viewing the array of visual displays of fashion apparel, women tend to compare idealized body images not only on virtual platforms of the brands but also on social media channels such as Instagram, which significantly increases their confidence toward buying such brands (McComb and Mills 2021).

Cognition and Reasoning

Visual reasoning provides comparison between the fashion objects and the self, which helps in deriving judgments on self-image congruence and materialistic differences. The personality attributes and qualitative representations of fashion anchors exhibiting the array of products also drive a visual reasoning challenge and inculcate perceptions toward *me-too feeling*. One of the major challenges in cognitive reasoning and judgments is managing multiple visual tasks on virtual platforms and comparing with the satisfaction on body image and social self-concepts. Consequently, comparing structural representations of visual displays and perceptual representations of subjects are complex, as they initially provide symbolic abstractions which requires self and peer conformity. Consumers exploring fashion apparel on virtual platforms use structural mapping of the visuals to derive appropriate judgments by comparing two product descriptions placing them in diverse alignments, which develops perceptions across visual arrays. Such structural mapping also supports the analogies to reinforce arousal and merriment toward buying fashion apparel (Rajagopal and Rajagopal 2023).

Arousal during virtual shopping is seeded by multilayer visual effects, which drive synchronous and asynchronous emotions in the context of social and personal appearance value. The visual effects of apparel display on virtual platforms develop impulse and arousal toward unplanned purchases. The gender, age, and the clarity in visual reasoning does not intervene in hindering emotions during time spent on browsing categorical images and animations driving fashion impulse among consumers. Retail technology has significantly contributed to improving the performance of both online and offline channels. The digital retailing has significantly supported displaying the fashion apparel through virtual platforms to drive consumer experience through virtual merchandising practices. Retailers using hybrid technologies have modified retailing practices both at virtual and brick-and-mortar stores. However, the ease-of-use and value perceptions of consumers on using technology-led digital platforms, which simulates products through AI and VR applications and drives shopping orientation among consumers. The ease-of-use of technology delivers a seamless experience through viewing the products repeatedly on digital platforms and often challenge the consumer decision-making in the context of analyzing utilitarian versus hedonic experiences. The compulsive attitude of consumers to viewing virtual merchandise moderates the effects of appearance similarity, product quality, and social value expectancy. The online shopping attractions have led to the new potential behavioral addictions resulting into continuous viewing of fashion apparel on mobile applications and developing purchase intentions. Such behavior is associated with variety seeking behavior, coping with stress disorders, mood modifications, and contributing to self-esteem. Often, consumers feel recreational orientation in observing virtual merchandise, which drives positive influences and perceived experiences (Gori et al. 2022).

Digital retailing through attractive product displays stimulates consumers' perceived values toward both utilitarian and hedonic perceptions, which significantly impact their impulsive buying behavior on the e-commerce platforms dedicated to fashion products. The retail technology and the ambience of virtual stores significantly influence the perceived use value of virtual retailing technologies and drive utilitarian and hedonic values regardless of their generic buying behaviors, peer acceptance, and conventional wisdom. Reviewing the opinions of respondents, the consumer behavior toward buying fashion apparel on virtual platforms can be interpreted to determine personal values associated with impulsive buying is more concerned with articulated individual perceptions over conventional social values and wisdom. The respondents also revealed that retailing technology of virtual stores is acceptable irrespective of initial difficulties in browsing and checking-out the shopping cart (Rajagopal and Rajagopal 2023).

The internal factors that influence the perceptual process of consumers include propensity of consumer learning on the attributes of products, services, and brands in the market and social ambience. The capability of retaining perceived memories and associated emotions also drives the cognitive process among consumers toward validating their brand perceptions. The perception of consumers toward shopping is commonly influenced by the social psychodynamics, need, enthusiasm for experimentation, benefit seeking, and obsessive behavioral attributes. Thus, consumer perceptions influence consumer behavior with their ecosystem, which often creates *me too* feeling, and induces the pro-perception buying decisions. In addition, perceived benefits in terms of price, associated promotions, and perceived use value of products significantly influence purchase intention. Perceived consumers' effectiveness, occupation, and income level also have significant effect on confirming the positive consumer perception toward willingness to pay for the product of high-perceived value (Zhao et al. 2018). The consumer perceptions toward stores and brands are motivated by the assortment of products in the store, music, store ergonomics, and visual merchandising comprising display, color, and nonverbal information about the product. The cognitive processing styles, motivational interests and concerns; prioritization of personal values; and neurological structures and physiological functions of consumers broadly determine their cognitive process in developing perception on the products and services. Companies need to analyze the perceptual maps of consumers to measure the intensity of their persuasion by developing appropriate strategies for advertising and communication. To analyze the consumers' perceptions and judgment to support their decision-making process, consumer-centric companies offer an array of consumer choice, product performance reviews over the social media (Jost 2017). Self-enhancement by acquiring knowledge and shared experiences on products and services helps consumers in developing sustainable perceptions to make right purchase intentions and buying decisions. Social networking sites such as Facebook or Twitter (now X) serve as an interesting platform in self-enhancement process, which enables consumers to compare different goals and behaviors over a predetermined mindset. Social media is an attractive platform where consumers with a changing mindset interact with peers demonstrating their perceptual rationale and validate their feelings and emotions. Their objective in engaging in social media is to learn about recent trends, new development of knowledge, or certain skill sets for further improvement in making buying decisions (Mathur et al. 2016).

Behavioral Proximity

The concept of proximity in businesses rose into prominence by the end of the 20th century, as crowd workspaces and sharing of experience offered deep and meaningful relationships between customers and employees of the company to increase the collective psychodynamics. Activities performed by firms in developing a new customer relationship are often built around efficient communication tasks to drive interpersonal communications, confidence, and cognitive bonding (Yamkovenko & Tavares, 2017). Brand marketing is characterized by extensive interpersonal communications not only between buyers and sellers but also between a wide variety of functions performed by the actors at back- and front-stages (Rajagopal 2011). Conversational interaction is an important tool to develop proximity and can be achieved by understanding how companies can forge authentic and durable brand relationships with various segments of consumers when they aggregate geographic marketing. Such interactions allow firms to not only understand customer insights but also realize the power of cocreation and coevolution of business in the competitive marketplace. A hybrid conversational-communication style drives positive customer–brand relationships and helps firms to evaluate the geodemographic association of brands with consumers. Firms can develop proximity index based on communication, interactivity, cognitive variables, relationship drivers, competitive touchpoints, and business growth. In addition, cocreating customer service and relationship hubs fosters marketing, public relations, and communications strategies to develop a positive consumer–business helix and ecosystem. This book argues that until companies understand the contribution of effective communications and relationship management, true growth in business is unlikely.

Market trends and consumer behavior are rapidly changing, and social media is playing a critical role in determining marketing decisions. Volatility of consumer markets can have significant negative effects on market share, profitability, and brand equity of companies. However, volatility is an embedded attribute of the competitive growth theory. The argument central to the theory of change management is that the companies operating in a competitive business environment consider consumer preferences, innovation, technology, and growth-related investments as dynamic variables. Customer-centric companies, therefore, tend to build simpler products to help consumers choose the right product. Creating interactive platforms and engaging customers and stakeholders in marketing products and services help companies transform conventional marketing practices to interactive and proximity-based BMs. Successful consumer marketing companies function on the "hub and spoke" model in developing relationships through influencer–member exchange (IMX) process to stay need-based and customer-centric in business. The changing media and consumption behaviors of consumers and skepticism toward traditional forms of advertising have prompted the growth of influencer marketing, which is an outgrowth of the proximity marketing concept. The critical impact of IMX depends on the interplay of key influencer characteristics and marketing disclosures. The growing changes in consumer behavior correspond partly with the rise of influencer marketing, defined as a tactic in which companies pay people (influencers), financially or in-kind, to produce social media content on behalf of the brands and influence consumers' preferences and purchase decisions. Consequently, the congruence of influencer attributes with consumers' cognition and reasoning abilities drives higher IMX effects. Consumers expect influencers to share insights on their experience and recommendations about latest trends to change preconceived notions and behavioral stigma (Audrezet et al., 2020).

Customer-centric firms largely support decision-making, idea-sharing, and emotions in managing business by engaging consumers in the strategy development process. Such companies develop abilities to fight conscious and unconscious biases as they coevolve with people and society. Social interactions often promote sustainable and social consumption of products. The interplay of consumers within the social (interpersonal) and digital (remote response) platforms also helps companies to adapt to inclusive BMs and stay distinctive in the competitive marketplace. Consumers today are increasingly looking for brands that have a social purpose above functional and competitive benefits. As a result, most companies are taking social stand in highly visible ways. An effective, convergent business strategy creates social and customer values by coevolving the brand in society. The network among society, people, and business stimulates cocreation and collective business designing. Convergence of society and business can be better understood by converging crowd perspectives, IMX factors, and continuous learning about consumer behavior and competitive growth perspectives (Kingston et al., 2019).

Value is often measured in either economic or social terms. The blended-value proposition emphasizes that true customer value, which is a blend of economic, social, and environmental components, is indivisible. After the success of networking practices of business activities with social media over decades, profit-seeking firms have laid explicit emphasis on the creation of strategic social value. This business philosophy has grown in nonprofit organizations as well. Social values are dynamic, and customer-centric companies continuously monitor the perpetual changes in social values, culture, and ethnicity. Consequently, companies adapt to the triadic philosophy of gaining social insights, blending business values in society, and cocreating innovative socio-business strategies to drive businesses deep into the social environment. The best practices reveal that these elements boost business performance by enhancing social values and narrowing consumer disparities.

Consumer perceptions, attitude, physiological needs, endogenous elements, and exogenous factors associated with companies and markets constitute consumer behavior over a long time. Consumer-centric companies periodically map behavioral patterns of consumers by understanding major perceptional and attitudinal patterns and interpreting them to develop appropriate marketing strategies. However, consumer behavior is sensitive to social dominance, self-esteem and self-actualization, hedonic values, and vogue in the marketplace. Therefore, it can be argued that personality is a highly relevant factor in determining consumer behavior on product choices and buying decisions. Most companies continuously provide stimuli to consumers and prompt their response. Such practices make consumer behavior dynamic and agile. The positive stimulus–response behavior increases the likelihood of goal attainment and facilitates need satisfaction. Hence, most consumers follow the guided path of marketers and respond to the given stimuli to gain desired satisfaction (Rajagopal 2018).

It has always been an advantage for retailers to penetrate in multicultural consumer segments in order to develop consumer behavior for ethnic products through competitive pricing and packaging strategies. Such consumer-centric strategies are even more valuable in creating and supporting multicultural marketing efforts for global companies trying to go local. However, one marketing strategy does not fit consumers of all cultural segments, as what may be appealing to one culture might have the opposite effect on another. Thus, ethnic marketing is sometimes challenging, as several factors like consumption behavior, social and family culture, beliefs, and personal values intervene in buying decisions. The distinctiveness of cultural features like social media reviews is profoundly associated with emotional expressions that play a significant role in buying behavior among consumers. The purchase behavior of young consumers is found to be homogeneous throughout the different ethnic consumer segments across the markets. However, there are some differences in this generation due to technology, social media interactions, and wider experience on consumption (Rajagopal and Castaño 2015).

Cognitive Analytics of Consumers

Motivations among consumers are intrinsic and extrinsic in nature. For example, extrinsic motivations for shopping might include the total ambience of shopping mall, layout, and extent of involvement in the shopping process. Ambience of shopping mall, architecture, ergonomics, variety, and excitement motivate the shopper to stay long and make repeated visits to the mall. Visual effects and economic advantages associated with promotional products in retail stores often stimulate compulsive buying behavior. Point-of-sales brochures, catalogues, and posters build assumption on perceived use value and the motivational relevance of buying decisions about a product. Emotional visuals exhibited on contextual factors, such as proximity or intensity of stimulus, drive perceptual and subjective reactions on utility and expected satisfaction about products.

Buying motivation among consumers might also emerge in view of the functional values (perceived use value, longevity of product, and value for money); aesthetic or emotional values of products, like product attraction and metaphoric concerns; and situational concerns, where consumers feel a product is attractive or worth buying because of promotional offers or irresistible price discounts on offer by the seller. Social referrals and curiosity also motivate consumers to develop purchase intentions and attitude toward brands over time (Sheth et al. 2011). A study on cigarette smoking found that consumers adapt to the aesthetic/emotional motives to decide whether or not to smoke. The social psychology on smoking motivates or demotivates consumers in getting associated with such consumption practice. Consumers need to justify their perception before giving in to motivations and making appropriate decision. Feeling intelligent, feeling confident, or feeling safe might be the right justification criteria to make the decision about whether or not to smoke. Unless regulated by government, companies generally offer unclassified and uniform motivations to consumers irrespective of personalized filtering criteria such as age, gender, income, and occupation. In addition to the motivational norms for consumers, challenge in the society, or failing to do somewhat different, also motivates consumers to adapt to smoking attitude. However, the intention to quit smoking can also be dominated by emotional motives, like fear of getting cancer, or dissonance in the family (Kees et al. 2010).

Consumer motivations are also egocentric and altruistic. Egocentric motivations are associated with self-esteem and social value and lead to stature differentiation, like a "face in the crowd." Premier and exclusive brands like Giorgio Armani induce egocentric motivation among consumers, which claims that every suit piece fabricated for men is unique as no identical piece of fabric can be found within the brand. Such motivation among consumers provides high satisfaction of being unique in the society and having an exclusive, a cut-above-the-rest kind of stature in the society. Consumers respond to altruistic motivations often by going beyond their economic capability to acquire products for the satisfaction of family and friends. Altruism is a cognitive process of acting out of concern for the well-being of others, without regard to one's self-interest. Altruism can be understood in a behavioral or a psychological sense. Motivationally, altruism is the desire to enhance the welfare of others at a net welfare loss to oneself. Behaviorally, altruism is any act that could have resulted from altruistic motivations. For example, consumers tend to buy suburban vehicles for the safety of children and family, though it might not serve the purpose of the owner. Similarly, sometimes working consumers may intend to purchase large-screen televisions more for the satisfaction of children and family than for their own. Among other motivations, economic pragmatism seems to play a much larger role than pure altruism when it comes to purchasing decisions. Therefore, companies seeking to exploit altruism to advance their sustainability agendas may need to rethink their approach and focus on offering tangible value that benefits the families and peers of altruistic consumers (Barcelona 2011).

Most people justify their purchases on social or economic grounds. For example, buying an expensive car, a house, or high-value high-tech electronics may be justified as a social need, and the motivation to make such a purchase decision can be validated by the desire to achieve a level of social status or economic equity that is at par with peers. In this case, buying motives are typically based on need, positive peer reviews, product is a test winner, or the product has positive price–quality ratio. However, the motivation to buy a high-tech, high-value product is drawn from the community. Emotional motives are often unconscious and connected with self-image, identity, interests, and affinity. Under emotional motive, individuals tend to override the associated rationale but justify the needs involuntarily and prejudicially to boost their self-esteem.

Immersive Experience

Immersive experience is largely driven by the visual impact of technology in marketing. It is a way to make someone feel like they are part of a different environment than their normal surroundings. Immersion can also be explained like the self-image congruence. This can be achieved by embedding the physical environment with sensory audiovisual contents in brain to develop cognitive reasoning based on the dictum of seeing is believing and experiencing. Augmented reality (AR), virtual reality (VR), and metaverse BMs offer an immersive experience to consumers. As technology in the area of immersive experience grew, MXR has risen to prominence because of the availability of hardware that integrates the advantages that come with experience-led business modeling. To provide an immersive and innovative technological solution for consumers and brands, most firms implement MXR. This technology is promising to transform BMs and consumer behavior. Several research studies have revealed how MXR boosts consumer engagement and purchase intentions (Nasr and El-Deeb 2023).

Firms adapting to innovative marketing practices leverage AR to craft immersive brand experiences by creating or cocreating (with consumers and suppliers) interactive advertising to enable consumers experience products and spaces in innovative ways. AR is the practice of displaying digital information over the real-time view of objects, people, or spaces in the physical world and plays a valuable role in integrated marketing programs. However, firms continue to explore best practices in this case and are in pursuit of ways to effectively implement AR programs in the marketplace. Consequently, there exists a gap in a framework that describes the active and passive ingredients of AR, but AR processes can help marketers to optimize their AR campaigns and enhance various types of consumer engagements, including user–brand, user–user, and user–bystander engagements (Scholz and Smith 2016). Despite challenges in implementing AR to create an immersive experience among consumers, firms facilitate consumer engagement by enabling users to interact with the digital content, other users, and nonparticipants in the AR experience.

In the print AR paradigm, firms like IKEA publish promotional digital magazine that is augmented with furniture, projecting it into a user's room, to help the user decide where and how best to place the piece of furniture that they seek to evaluate before placing an order; another example is the Cadbury Quack Smack, in which a package of a chocolate bar is augmented with an interactive game. Geolayering is also a part of AR technology, which explains augmenting the space around the user with digital objects that may or may not be linked to specific geo-locations, typically using privately owned devices triggered by the user. For example, using Kringle Santa Claus application parents can create artifacts providing evidence of Santa Claus visiting the home. Magic mirroring of objects is another approach supported by the technology used in AR. It is all about augmenting the space or objects around the user with digital objects, which typically include public digital screen and television screens that can be disguised as normal mirrors. The user can see themselves as part of the augmentation, either in direct view in a digital mirror or by watching their actions on a screen as a third person (Nasr and El-Deeb 2023).

The AR experience on mobile devices is usually initiated for the user to experience AR effects through the *bogus window*, which refers to a virtual window that is generated on a device's screen, appearing as if it is a real-world window through which the user can see augmented content overlaid onto the actual surroundings. Essentially, it is a visual placeholder that frames the AR elements within the real-world view, allowing for a more intuitive user experience. The design of a bogus window is intended to create the illusion of looking through a real opening often with visual cues like borders, shadows, and perspective to enhance realism. A toy manufacturer can use a bogus window on a mobile application to allow customers to virtually play with a toy in their living room by viewing it through the phone's screen as if looking through a real window. LEGO has used AR to make its building blocks more interactive since 2018. LEGO AR toys use a special base and application to scan a physical set and bring it to life. The AR features include animations, games, and challenges. However, sometimes the augmentation occurs behind the bogus window, where the user cannot see themselves as part of the augmentation. Immersive experience through AR is also used in the tourism industry. The Chengdu Research Base of Giant Panda Breeding (Panda Base), located in Chengdu, China, was the world's most popular scenic spot for giant panda tourism. The Panda Base began to build panda culture and the panda brand to resolve low brand awareness and to better protect the giant panda. In 2020, Panda Base promoted the giant panda on various digital media platforms. Based on the concept of Web 3.0 and with the 5G technology, the Panda Base integrated social media marketing, content marketing, and viral marketing to promote panda culture and brand value and successfully developed its core cultural brand value (Zhao et al. 2020).

Potentially, immersive technology can reshape storytelling and reporting processes by putting people at the center of big events and issues, which makes journalism today more impressive and memorable than is possible with conventional approach. Therefore, news outlets like *New York Times*, *Washington Post*, and *Guardian* are using VR, 360-degree videos, and AR to engage readers and build empathy with them (Haddow and Haddow 2023). Technologies inculcating immersive experiences in commerce have several attributes that influence transformative shopping emotions and behavior. Some of such attributes are discussed below:

- Immersive technology supported by AR enhances product visualization and engagement. Immersive shopping allows customers to interact with product information in a more tangible and meaningful way. It allows customers to visualize products in their own environment or on themselves, reducing uncertainty in the perceived use value of products (McCabe and Castel, 2008).
- It offers personalized and memorable experiences by understanding customer preferences and behaviors. Accordingly, brands can be articulated to provide more customized recommendations, offer virtual trial sessions, and showcasing interactive product demonstrations. Such personalization not only enhances customer engagement with brands but also builds stronger emotional

connections with brands and products that drive brand loyalty in the long term.

- Immersive experience driven by AR offers global proximity and accessibility to customers across the e-commerce firms to navigate, buy, and get deliveries of their order.
- Immersive shopping allows customers to explore virtual showrooms, participate in live shopping events, and interact with brands simultaneously in a real-time environment.

To implement immersive technology, firms need to make efforts to understand customers' response to immersive experiences and how AR works in enhancing the impact on business. Accordingly, AR-powered virtual pilot project can be initiated by aspiring firms. However, interactive product videos are a good plan to start with to experiment the effect of AR. E-commerce firms use live shopping platforms for real-time engagement, and these platforms enable firms to host real-time product demonstrations, conduct interactive sessions, and offer exclusive promotions. Metaverse technology is a collection of technologies that enable the creation of virtual 3D worlds where users can interact, work, learn, and more. The metaverse is a concept that refers to a collective virtual shared space created by the convergence of virtually enhanced physical and digital reality. It is often described as the next iteration of the Internet, where users can be represented by avatars and interact in immersive 3D environment.

Multichannel Marketing

E-commerce business is expanding with multichannel marketing today, which refers to a strategy where an online retailer sells their products across multiple digital channels, through their own website, social media platforms, online marketplaces (like Amazon), and potentially physical kiosks and retail stores to enhance outreach and increase sales. Multichannel marketing by e-commerce firms is about selling products on various partner platforms instead of relying solely on one online storefront. Exploring the market through partner channels enables firms to connect with customers, potentially tapping into new demographics and customer segments of their partner firms. This strategy allows for selling on platforms like Instagram, Facebook, eBay, and dedicated online stores, providing more options for customers to purchase. As customers find their products on preferred channels and buy a product on their preferred platform, it leads to convenience and high shopping experience. Various clothing brands are shown in a firm's website by showcasing products on Instagram with shoppable posts and listing items on Amazon Marketplace. These firms also place targeted advertisements on Facebook and on the large e-commerce firms like Amazon.

Social media channels constitute one of the major outlets for product marketing. A multichannel marketing strategy involves interacting with customers consistently on more than one channel, such as a mobile app or a website, e-mail, SMS, social media, and pay-per-click. Implementing a solid multichannel marketing strategy is crucial for e-commerce growth. A resilient e-commerce business is commonly based on the following attributes of business diversification:

- Channel Diversity: A competitive strategy to list and advertise products across multiple channels, including digital and physical marketplaces, trendy kiosks, and search engines including the website of the e-commerce firm.
- Fulfillment Diversity: Expanding the inventory, logistics, and shipping capabilities to ensure efficient delivery of products to customers in both B-to-B and B-to-C segments.
- Geographical Diversity: Exploring demand for products in multiple markets through international partnerships with collaborative distributors to support retailers in geodemographic marketplaces.
- Supply Chain Diversity: Mitigate risk by creating backup plans for procurement, manufacturing, and inventory management.

Adding new channels to e-commerce network includes both vertical (product-mix) and horizontal (geodemographic) strategies to increase consumer proximity and optimize customer journey and creating a resilient distribution. Implementing this strategy requires a methodical approach to launch products in different channels successfully. A new channel takes a long time to demonstrate efficiency and confidence among consumers, which may need the firms to meticulously develop the blueprint of multichannel operations to achieve a win-win business performance.

To develop a successful multichannel marketing strategy bridging inter-firm connections is an important requirement. Channel partners' exploring and reviewing of channel requirements enables e-commerce or hybrid firms to build connections for efficient inventory management, product information, and ongoing monitoring after launching the products. Marketing efficiency across channels can be achieved through campaigns that ensure the visiting of products and sales take-off dynamics. Multichannel marketing encourages joint sales operations with partner channels. Therefore, one of the major challenges is managing and consolidating inventory on multiple channels. Consequently, firms can ensure inventory replenishments and avoid out-of-stock situations in fulfilling customer orders. Firms also need to be robust in implementing multichannel marketing to create compelling product listings on partner channels' pages on Facebook and Instagram as a part of social media network. Listing products in multiple channels has a major task of aligning prices with similar products listed in other channels to stay competitive, visible, and profitable. Firms operating in multiple channels must develop fulfillment options following the requirements of the channel and prepare to meet consumer expectations for timely communication and delivery of orders. Multichannel marketing activities such as procurement, manufacturing, distribution, inventory management, and logistics make the optimization of these processes challenging. However, through AI-based monitoring, analysis of key performance indicators and creative insights contributes significantly to increasing the channel's performance.

Case Study

CS1 Pinduoduo: E-commerce with Social Values in China

Pinduoduo is a Chinese e-commerce company that primarily focuses on a group-buying model, allowing users to purchase items at discounted prices by forming groups with other buyers; it is considered one of the fastest-growing e-commerce platforms in China, often competing with giants like Alibaba and JD.com. This company was created by Colin

Huang in 2015. Users can download the Pinduoduo app on their smartphone or access the platform via its website. Pinduoduo went public on the NASDAQ stock market in the United States, raising US$1.6 billion through an IPO in the U.S. market (Initial Public Offering). This made it one of the largest IPOs in 2018 (Lau and Zhu 2018). The core feature of Pinduoduo is the ability to get lower prices by inviting friends to join a group purchase. Users can share deals with friends on social media to encourage group buying. Pinduoduo operates the *Temu* platform for international markets, including the United States. The company has seen significant user growth since its launch, becoming a major player in the Chinese e-commerce market.

Amid the Covid-19 pandemic, Pinduoduo's agile response to the crisis and its corporate social initiatives on rural revitalization in China gained enormous social value. Established in 2015 in Shanghai, Pinduoduo's has grown as the third-largest shopping platform in China within the first 3 years of its founding. Valued at an estimated US$63 billion in May 2020, the NASDAQ-listed technology company had pursued an innovative concept of team purchase, coupled with social sharing, viral marketing, and gamification as its growth and user engagement strategies. A key part of Pinduoduo's initial user acquisition was targeting the untapped rural market. In giving back to society, the company created a meaningful impact on farmers' livelihoods. The firm has developed agriculture with an Internet model that enabled growers to bypass unnecessary intermediaries to reach consumers' markets rapidly and profitably. Poverty-stricken farmers who participated in the *Duo Duo Farm* program had the opportunity to attend entrepreneurship training and obtain subsidies, resources, and advice. *Duo Duo Farm* initiative has been driven by Pinduoduo, which aimed at empowering small-scale farmers in rural areas by connecting them directly with consumers through their platform, allowing farmers to sell their produce at better prices while also providing them with training, support, and access to technology to improve their farming practices and alleviate poverty in rural communities. The *Farm-to-Consumer* business model focused on agricultural development and rural economic growth. Through these collective social initiatives, farmers in China have moved forward with improved productivity, higher-quality products, and increased incomes. During the COVID-19 outbreak, Pinduoduo stepped in to support farmers' sales of agricultural produce on its livestreaming channels (Liang and Mei 2020).

Pinduoduo's business model is primarily based on social e-commerce maxim, where users are incentivized to invite friends and family to join group purchases. This allows them to access significantly discounted prices on products by leveraging the power of social sharing, primarily through WeChat. This drives user acquisition and engagement, while focusing on a consumer-to-manufacturer (C2M) model to offer lower prices on commodity-oriented goods. The firm functions as a group-buying strategy and demonstrates its core feature as the ability of users and their families and friends to purchase items on-farm at significantly lower prices offered by the farmers that helps the firm reach a certain quantity threshold. Users are encouraged to share product links on social media platforms like *WeChat*—a popular smartphone-based communication application in China—to invite others to join group purchases, boosting user acquisition and engagement. The company heavily leverages the mobile app experience, integrating seamlessly with popular messaging platforms like WeChat. Pinduoduo connects consumers directly with manufacturers eliminating middlemen and allowing for lower prices, which not only offers price competitiveness but also helps the company improve customer loyalty. The company focuses on value-for-money products to offer high satisfaction and perceived use value on buying products. Periodically, Pinduoduo offers rewards like discounts and cash-back for inviting friends to the platform and participating in group buys. The fast-growing company allows consumers to group together to get better discounts from merchants selling goods as varied as clothes, kitch-enware, and gadgets. Due to low-priced products and a large user base in China's smaller cities, the firm's gross merchandise volume exceeded 100 billion yuan (approximately US$14.98 billion) last year. Alibaba's Taobao marketplace took 5 years to reach that milestone, while JD.com took a decade (Lau and Zhu 2018).

Pinduoduo generates revenue through commissions on sales and advertising. The primary source of revenue for the company is taking a commission on each transaction made on the platform. Merchants can pay to promote their products through targeted advertising on the platform. Pinduoduo's social shopping model has significantly disrupted the Chinese e-commerce landscape by tapping into a new market of price-conscious consumers. This e-commerce company serves largely the lower demographic consumer profiles. The e-commerce platform of Pinduoduo is particularly popular among lower-income groups in China due to its focus on affordable goods. However, a major dilemma prevails around the business growth of Pinduoduo—that is, how could the company strike a balance between its sustainability efforts and the pursuit of its core business as an e-commerce platform as the country gradually emerged from the COVID-19 pandemic?

Summary

Discussions in this chapter focus on the impact of ICT on consumer behavior, which has been the driving force in the success of digital networks and e-commerce with the emergence of AI and machine learning. Thematic discussions are knitted around the technosocial shifts as a key driver impacting virtual consumer behavior by guiding consumer cognition and reasoning toward virtual engagement. The platform economy has shown a huge shift in the creation of consumer value. The platform economy has a distinct set of business and economic relations that depend on the Internet, computation, and data. Consumer experience is diffused by user-generated content on social media, which helps them to review consumer perceptions, attitude, and behavior toward a brand in the marketplace. The behavioral alignment of needs and product displays in stores refers to the psychological and cognitive processes involved in buying behavior. Consumers prioritize convenience to seek seamless experiences across devices and platforms. This includes easy navigation, quick checkouts, flexible payment options, and guaranteed reverse logistics. E-commerce firms encourage omnichannel marketing, and shoppers expect a consistent experience through shopping online, on mobile apps or in physical stores.

Virtual shopping allows customers to browse products online as they would in a physical store. Such shopping facilities can include features like 3D product views, virtual try-ons, and interactive catalog. The chapter argues that patterns of consumerism are changing in the society, as there are shifts in consumer demography in the global marketplace. The virtual merchandising on digital platforms drives self-endorsement and predetermined psychological effects induced by collective intelligence and hedonic disposition. Deliberations on the impact of technology on consumer behavior highlight the changing techno-behavioral paradigm in shopping among consumers. One of the major impacts of retail digital technologies are the 3V factors—comprising value creation, value delivery, and value capture. Both AI and virtual reality (VR) support the consumer's learning process in relation to product design, attributes, and values and help consumers make appropriate buying decisions in quick time. The chapter also discusses the concept of behavioral proximity in e-commerce and immersive experience of consumers in digital shopping aided by AR and VR technologies. A hybrid conversational-communication style drives positive customer–brand relationships and helps firms evaluate the geodemographic association of brands with consumers. Overall, discussion on customer-centric virtual market system with a focus on consumer outreach, business expansion, and innovation and technology is central to this chapter, with the discussion bringing a specific focus on holistic perspectives of behavioral engagement. The hybrid BMs integrating the cyber–physical infrastructure meet the increasing challenges of the changing market ecosystem. In addition, other main topics discussed in this chapter include marketing value matrix, multichannel marketing, and 3T elements comprising time, trust, and transparency that significantly affect the virtual marketing process. The chapter ends with a case study on the Chinese e-commerce company Pinduoduo focusing on Pinduoduo's mission to create social values through virtual business in the rural regions of China.

References

Audrezet, A., G. de Kerviler, and J. G. Moulard. 2020. "Authenticity Under Threat: When Social Media Influencers Need to Go Beyond Self-Presentation." *Journal of Business Research* 117: 557–69.

Barcelona, R. G. 2011. "New Tools to Capture the Elusive Green Consumer." *IESE-Insight Magazine* First Quarter (8): 21–8.

Capatina, A., M. Kachour, J. Lichy, A. Micu, A. E. Micu, and F. Codignola. 2020. "Matching the Future Capabilities of an Artificial Intelligence-Based Software for Social Media Marketing with Potential Users' Expectations."

Technological Forecasting and Social Change 151: 119794. https://doi.org/10.1016/j.techfore.2019.119794.

Gori, A., E. Topino, and S. Casale. 2022. "Assessment of Online Compulsive Buying: Psychometric Properties of the Italian Compulsive Online Shopping Scale (COSS)." *Addictive Behaviors* 129: 107274. https://doi.org/10.1016/j.addbeh.2022.107274.

Grewal, D., D. K. Gauri, A. L. Roggeveen, and R. Sethuraman. 2021. "Strategizing Retailing in the New Technology Era." *Journal of Retailing* 97 (1): 6–12.

Haddow, G. D., and K. S. Haddow. 2023. "Technology Is Driving Changes in Disaster Communications." In *Disaster Communications in a Changing Media World*, edited by G. D. Haddow and K. S. Haddow. Oxford, UK: Butterworth-Heinemann.

Jost, J. 2017. "The Marketplace of Ideology: 'Elective Affinities' in Political Psychology and Their Implications for Consumer Behavior." *Journal of Consumer Psychology* 27 (4): 502–20.

Karagür, Z., J. M. Becker, K. Klein, and A. Edeling. 2022. "How, Why, and When Disclosure Type Matters for Influencer Marketing." *International Journal of Research in Marketing* 39 (2): 313–35.

Kees, J., S. Burton, J. Andrews, and J. Kozup. 2010. "Understanding How Graphic Pictorial Warnings Work on Cigarette Packaging." *Journal of Public Policy & Marketing* 29 (2): 265–76.

Lau, F., and J. Zhu. 2018. "China's Pinduoduo Prices U.S. IPO at Top of Range, Raises $1.6 Billion: Sources." Reuters, July 26. https://www.reuters.com/article/us-pinduoduo-ipo/chinas-pinduoduo-prices-us-ipo-at-top-of-range-raises-16-billion-sources-idUSKBN1KG05J/.

Liang, H., and C. S. Mei. 2020. "Pinduoduo: Empowering Farmers with an e-Commerce Platform." *Asian Management Insights* 7 (2): 44–51. https://cmp.smu.edu.sg/sites/cmp.smu.edu.sg/files/ami/8_AMI14_PinDuoDuo.pdf.

Mathur, P., H. H. Chun, and D. Maheswaran. 2016. "Consumer Mindsets and Self-Enhancement: Signaling Versus Learning." *Journal of Consumer Psychology* 26 (1): 142–52.

McCabe, D. P., and A. D. Castel. 2008. "Seeing Is Believing: The Effect of Brain Images on Judgments of Scientific Reasoning." *Cognition* 107 (1): 343–52.

McComb, S.E. and Mills, J.E. (2021), "Young women's body image following upwards comparison to Instagram models: The role of physical appearance perfectionism and cognitive emotion regulation", *Body Image*, Vol. 38, pp. 49-62.

Nasr, R. S., and S. El-Deeb. 2023. "Exploring Mixed Reality: Enhancing Consumer Interaction." In *Confronting Security and Privacy Challenges in Digital Marketing*, edited by P. Pires, J. Santos, I. Pereira, and A. Torres. IGI Global Scientific Publishing.

Rajagopal. 2011. "The Symphony Paradigm: Strategy for Managing Market Competition." *Journal of Transnational Management* 16 (3): 181–99.

Rajagopal. 2018. *Consumer Behavior Theories: Convergence of Divergent Perspectives with Applications to Marketing and Management.* New York: Business Expert Press.

Rajagopal. 2021. *The Business Design Cube: Converging Markets, Society, and Customer Values to Grow Competitive in Business.* New York: Business Expert Press.

Rajagopal, and R. Castaño. 2015. *Understanding Consumer Behaviour and Consumption Experience.* Hershey, PA: IGI Global.

Rajagopal, and A. Rajagopal. 2023. "'Seeing Is Experiencing': Impact of Showcasing Fashion Merchandise on Digital Platforms." *Qualitative Market Research* 26 (3): 214–31.

Riegger, A. S., J. F. Klein, K. Merfeld, and S. Henkel. 2021, "Technology-Enabled Personalization in Retail Stores: Understanding Drivers and Barriers." *Journal of Business Research* 123: 140–55.

Scholz, J., and A. N. Smith. 2016. "Augmented Reality: Designing Immersive Experiences That Maximize Consumer Engagement." *Business Horizons* 59 (2): 149–61.

Sheth, J. N., N. K. Sethia, and S. Srinivas. 2011. "Mindful Consumption: A Customer-Centric Approach to Sustainability." *Journal of the Academy of Marketing Science* 39 (1): 21–39.

Song, S. Y., and Y. K. Kim. 2020. "Factors Influencing Consumers' Intention to Adopt Fashion Robot Advisors: Psychological Network Analysis." *Clothing and Textiles Research Journal* 40 (1): 3–18.

Yamkovenko, B., and S. Tavares. 2017. *To Understand Whether Your Company Is Inclusive, Map How Your Employees Interact.* Harvard Business Review Digital Article. Cambridge, MA: Harvard Business School Press.

Zha, D., Foroudi, P., Melewar, T.C. and Jin, Z. (2022), "Experiencing the Sense of the Brand: The Mining, Processing and Application of Brand Data Through Sensory Brand Experiences." *Qualitative Market Research* 25 (2): 205–32.

Zhao, M., Y. Chen, C. Hsu, N. Su, and G. Tang. 2020. *Panda Base: Digital Transformation for Wildlife Conservation.* Cambridge, MA: Harvard Business School Publishing.

Zhao, R., Y. Geng, Y. Liu, X. Tao, and B. Xue. 2018. "Consumers' Perception, Purchase Intention, and Willingness to Pay for Carbon-Labeled Products: A Case Study of Chengdu in China." *Journal of Cleaner Production* 171 (1): 1664–71.

CHAPTER 5

Virtual Branding

Overview

Virtual branding is central to conversations and arguments about e-commerce. The chapter portrays virtual brand advocacy through experiential marketing, collective consumerism, advocacy patterns, and future shopping trends. Building acquaintance with virtual brands, developing brand communities, and architecting crowd-based branding are some of the topics discussed in this chapter. Discussions on developing online brands and launching virtual brands to create a tangible effect as the top-of-the-mind brands are central to this chapter. In addition, challenges and competitive strategies concerning online brand positioning and value creation among consumers are discussed. Cocreation as a customer-centric branding strategy for e-commerce brands has been discussed at length in this chapter.

Developing Online Brands

Virtual branding is all about the firms creating a strong and engaging online presence for their brand. It involves using digital and immersive technologies to build and maintain the brand's identity, connect with their audience, and stand out in a crowded digital marketplace. Immersive experience emerges largely with the digital branding approach in e-commerce firms. This includes creating a distinctive logo, engaging color palettes, and expressive typography that are consistently applied across all digital platforms by utilizing AR and VR to create interactive and engaging brand experiences. AR can help customers visualize products in their own environment and generate significant customer value. Digital firms engaged in B-to-B, B-to-C, and hybrid marketing develop and post compelling narratives and high-quality content on product websites through online media such as storyboard, blog posts, videos, and infographics to attract and engage audience in order to reinforce the brand image and value. Such digital content helps e-commerce firms to use consumer data to create targeted campaigns that resonate with individual preferences, enhancing customer satisfaction and loyalty. In addition, firms benefit from social media participation by promoting active customer participation in conversations on various types of digital content, encouraging the customers to share or exchange their views on the firms' social media platforms and using the data generated from those views to fine-tune brand strategies by utilizing data research tools such as collective intelligence analytics. Digital brand development is also benefited by collaborating with social media influencers to reach new audiences and build and promote brand credibility. Building brands on digital platforms through user-generated content enables firms to encourage customers to share their experiences using a brand, which not only helps the firms in promoting the brand but also helps them in creating customer value. The multichannel consistency helps brands gain a seamless and consistent brand experience across all digital touchpoints from websites to social media platforms. Consequently, virtual branding allows firms to experiment with and redefine the brand identity in the digital space.

Consumer brands have benefited largely from the rapidly advancing technology leading to online shopping platforms that generated strong revenue growth through the virtual companies in online marketplaces such as Flipkart (India) and Amazon (United States, Mexico, India, and Europe). The powerful volume-driven online mass-shopping platforms have accounted for 80 percent of global online sales in 2014, which reflects in particular such firms' ability to exert greater control on user traffic in relation to consumer brands, product searches, or access to consumer data. Most of the large online sales platforms are brand-owned sites of multinational manufacturing and retailing companies like Procter & Gamble, Walmart, and many others. Their online sites share e-commerce with other service providers and retailers to enhance their brand and market outreach. In the United States, by contrast, though platforms such as Amazon Marketplace and eBay continue to increase their share, brand-owned and more brand-friendly online retailers, including those sites with limited control, account for about 70 percent of all e-commerce business (Bu 2015).

Camera IQ is a company that specializes in AR marketing. Founded in 2016 and based in Santa Monica, California, Camera IQ developed a platform that helps marketers create, manage, and measure AR campaigns. These campaigns are designed to engage a wider range of audiences across social media and streaming platforms. Camera IQ empowered brands to create and launch AR experiences across social media platforms and raised funds to further its product development and expand its virtual marketing and sales efforts. The company has also worked on democratizing its marketing activities, breaking down significant technological barriers to harness the power of AR in their digital marketing campaigns. The technology integrates various operating systems of the company, including AR toolkits and applications, to deliver captivating marketing experiences through smartphone cameras. Despite its emphasis on accelerating business growth, the company continues to face issues on how to segment and target their customer base to drive exponential growth and determine the most effective ways to direct its AI and engineering resources to refine their platform in order to meet the needs of an expanding and diversifying customer base. Camera IQ refined its customer value proposition by differentiating AR experiences and moving beyond traditional advertising to gain a richer, more immersive, and engaging brand experience (Avery and Nahas 2021).

The desire for developing online brands has been growing steadily since the mid-20th century. Since that time, the commercial use of Internet has been growing in a way that has belied all expectations and signifies its now-all-pervasive influence on both the society and global economy reflecting a manifold increase in its use in global e-commerce and across a wide range of consumer segments. Consumer-focused companies tend to build online brands to create awareness about the brand and the services associated with it for creating stronger perceptions among consumers. Some companies realize that putting resources on building online brands could meet consumer-focused goals better by providing them easy and interactive information online, which could help consumers persistently recognize a brand. Some companies argue in favor of integrating online branding from the point of view of providing overall brand experience to customers in relation to product attributes, brand equity, social status, economic power of the brand, services quality, and about the company itself in a competitive marketplace. From this perspective, online brand development and recognition are viewed as an integrated function of the company, which could help firms achieve significant product and brand differentiation vis-à-vis competing brands in the marketplace. Most companies operating through both online and brick-and-mortar stores seek to codesign their brands by engaging in dialog with consumers dynamically on social media. In the age of dynamic social media, brand dialogues are facilitated by Internet and mobile communications among consumers and help brands achieve high equity in the market. To promote brands appropriately online, developing a robust website is a key component in the company's growth initiatives. An attractive, easy-to-navigate website can present products and services in a way that brings in an exponential increase in the number of consumers visiting (hitting) the website to evaluate the brand. The overall appearance of the website, its contents, its interactivity, and company's messages on the website, all provide a positive experience to consumers who visit the online brands to gain more in-depth knowledge about products and services of the company. Companies also encourage consumer blogs to generate content for readers interested in topics related to the brands and the companies.

Online branding has become popular also in the local companies that are confined to specific language and sociodemographic niches. The branding and marketing strategy of the oldest ethnic comic-book series in India—Amar Chitra Katha (ACK)—has gone for reinforcing online branding that started in the millennium break (2001) as an educational tool to make Indian children aware of Indian mythology, history, and culture. ACK series had reached around 500 titles by 2010, covering a wide range of topics from history to mythology and stories on morality and ethics. However, due to animated television sitcoms, the behavior of reading comic books has been radically declining. Besides, because of animated television serials, ACK has been facing competition not only from international and indigenous comic-book companies but also from Internet such as children's online games. In November 2007, all of the ACK titles and Tinkle Magazine were bought by Mumbai-based entrepreneur Samir Patil, who created ACK Media as an umbrella brand. The company tried to reach its audience through the launch of an online portal, the creation of DVDs/VCDs, sponsoring movies based on ACK, placing comics on mobile electronic platforms, and so on. The shift from print media branding to online branding was inevitable for the company as it wanted to revive and reinforce the brand and rebuild a sustainable position of the brand in the marketplace. The decision of the company to develop online branding was also instrumental to achieving growth and maintaining brand equity in the marketplace. The company has introduced online shopping alongside its brand-building efforts on the virtual platform. ACK Media is India's leading entertainment and education company for young audiences. The company develops products for multiple platforms including print, home videos, television and films, and mobile and online services (Roy and Moorthi 2012).

Online branding, also known as Internet branding or e-branding, is the process of using the Internet and social media to create and promote an identity of a virtual brand. The synchronized way of developing a virtual brand for e-commerce firms requires going through the following stages:

- Defining a Right Brand: The foundation of a brand lies in the purpose of the brand with an emphasis on its personality, voice, and story. The brand personality is expressed through its voice, core values, beliefs, and visual identity. A brand voice should be consistent across all channels and reflect the corporate values. It should be unique to the company and help customers understand what to expect from both corporate and user-generated content, services, and customer service.
- Creating a Brand Style: Establish guidelines for the brand's visual and verbal elements, such as colors, typography, logos, and messaging. The brand style guidelines state the manner in which a virtual brand should be visually exhibited across all communication channels, including its colors, fonts, logo usage, imagery, and overall design aesthetic, ensuring consistency in how the brand is perceived by the public; essentially, it's a set of rules for maintaining a cohesive brand identity across different platforms.
- Designing Brand Assets: It is important in building virtual brands to create a memorable logo and other brand assets. Brand assets are elements that define a company's identity and help it stand

out from competitors. Brand assets are crucial for building brand identity, recognition, and loyalty. Brand asset management is the process of organizing, storing, and accessing brand assets in a centralized system to maintain consistent branding. The competitive brand assets include:

- Visual assets such as logo, color palettes, typography, packaging, imagery, and icons
- Verbal assets like brand slogans, taglines, and tone of voice;
- Auditory assets including jingles, voiceovers, and sound effects;
- Exclusive assets in the form of signature products, environments, or marketing materials;
- Tactile assets demonstrating the materials used in packaging, products, or retail environments;
- Symbolic assets encompassing brand emotions, use values, brand personality, and associated brand story;
- Digital assets that are illustrated on websites, social media profiles, and digital content like blogs and videos;
- Physical assets containing business cards, uniforms, and signage. Brand signage refers to visual display, like a sign or banner, which prominently features a company's logo, colors, and design elements, essentially acting as a physical representation of a brand identity and communicating its message to customers through visual cues;
- Press information and brand reviews as a collection of relevant articles, reviews, and interviews that highlight the brand's work;
- Highlights and achievements of the brand, which demonstrate the strength of the brands, such as accomplishments, awards, notable performances, and significant milestones; and
- Social media and livestreaming links associated with social media profiles and streaming platforms.

- Building a Brand Website: E-commerce firms can develop brand trust among consumers by developing a brand-specific website. Brand trust is built as consumers believe a company is safe to deal with and honest and reliable in delivering products with high quality and perceived value. Brand trust can be evaluated through the Net Promoters Score (NPS). A customer loyalty metric is calculated through NPS, which measures the likeliness of customers to recommend transacting with a company, product, or service to family, friends, peers, or the neighborhood or community to which they belong. NPS is calculated by subtracting the percentage of customers who are detractors from the percentage of those who are promoters. The resulting score ranges from −100 to +100, with higher scores being better. Commonly, the scores above zero are considered good, above 20 are favorable, and above 50 are excellent.

- Optimizing the Website: Investing in search engine optimization (SEO) is crucial to improve the website's ranking. Website optimization is the process of improving a website's performance to increase traffic, engagement, conversions, and revenue. It involves optimizing the speed of navigation, usability, conversion rates, SEO, and other relevant content. To achieve an effective SEO process, e-commerce firms should publish relevant, authoritative content that's easy to read and covers everything searchers want to know. Including a compelling title tag, key words, description and including enough current and backlinks will help firms optimize search engine performance. Creating and posting engaging content on the product and brand websites will also help optimize search engine performance through engaging in dialog online with the target audience.
- Creating Social Media Campaigns: Leverage social media marketing to reach target audience. Building relationships with customers through e-mail helps firms to enhance brand image and personality among consumers. Tracking brand mentions using data-text mining techniques is an essential strategy to humanize the brand and monitor the brand performance online.

Brands exploit social media extensively in the age of Internet to offer and communicate the company's promise to customers and build consumer trust. Consumer interactivity through various community forums like Facebook, Twitter (now X), and blogs continuously helps companies to refine the brand promise and exhibit innovative differentiation to drive sustainable association with customers. Virgin Atlantic scans travel websites to learn the voice of customers and includes travel tips from crew members on its Facebook page. The company keeps communicating with customers on Twitter (now X) on changing marketing and operational strategies to enhance its brand. It also maintains V-Travelled, a site where customers exchange their experience and advice fellow consumers while they plan a big trip. Companies gain customer insights through social media and online interactions and drive up sales performance capitalizing on the reach and popularity of social networks. However, companies need to take all possible care to protect their brand's reputation and carefully follow customer engagement rules online (Barwise and Meehan 2010).

Most multinational and local consumer products manufacturing companies have invested larger resources and expended more efforts by building communities around their brands to increase marketing efficiency and improve brand performance in order to create sustainable customer loyalty. However, it is important to meticulously organize brand communities and set clear protocols about their functions. Consumers interact online to share their experience, clarify fellow consumers' doubts, and resolve post-purchase problems of buyers within the brand community. Many companies dealing with consumer technology products like Apple Inc., Samsung, Cannon, Lexmark, Del Computers, Cannon, Sony, Harley-Davidson, and many others have created brand communities to promote and protect their brands with the help of consumers through online forums. Despite the popularity of brand communities and the role of consumers in serving these communities, there are some common misconceptions about the damages to the brands through undesired communication. Thus, companies also offer design principles, cautionary tales, and new approaches for leveraging those communities. Brand communities help companies develop marketing strategies and create optimal impact on managing performance against competing brands. Accordingly, as a corporate strategy, companies like Procter & Gamble and Unilever are hosting and promoting online brand communities for specific consumer brands from their product lineup. Companies engaged in fashion products like designer clothes, and challenging products like Harley-Davidson motorcycles redesigned their organizational policy to support building and maintaining its brand community and treated all community-related activities not just as marketing expenses but as a companywide investment and commitment. An effective brand community serves its members and shares knowledge and skills by building relationships, cultivating new interests, and contributing to society. Strong online communities consistently work toward developing an understanding of members' needs and engage them by offering a variety of roles (Fournier and Lee 2009).

Online branding has been driven by major global information technology giants—Google and Yahoo, for example—through various platforms as an active tool for generating awareness among consumers about brands, products, and services from emerging companies with enormous growth potential. The click-per-view advertisements and YouTube hosted brand communications to play an enormous role in stimulating interest, knowledge, and action among consumers to learn and act online about brands and companies of their choice. YouTube has become a massively popular site to host brands in an attractive manner. Building from user-generated content, YouTube has turned to experimenting with professionally made content and organizing its videos under various channels besides supporting general consumer-generated content. However, YouTube is yet to create clear-cut commercial policies about generating advertising revenue from its online video platform. This social video website is engaged in developing a "brand safe" platform that major marketers can use to promote their visual communication endeavors (Teixeira and Kornfeld 2014). Online branding follows an ecosystem comprising several factors from the perspectives of consumers and companies (see Figure 5.1).

The online branding ecosystem illustrated in Figure 5.1 reveals that from the consumers' point of view online branding is quite attractive as consumers can acquire adequate knowledge on product attributes and pricing and gain comparative awareness about similar brands online. As stated previously, online branding provides consumers with an opportunity to peer-review the brand and take enough time to make a decision. The virtual brand communities organized by companies help consumers to not only learn about the brand but also critically examine its use value and associated competitive advantages. Online branding is very cost-effective for the companies as their brands can tap a wide range of geodemographic segments of consumers. Companies develop exclusive

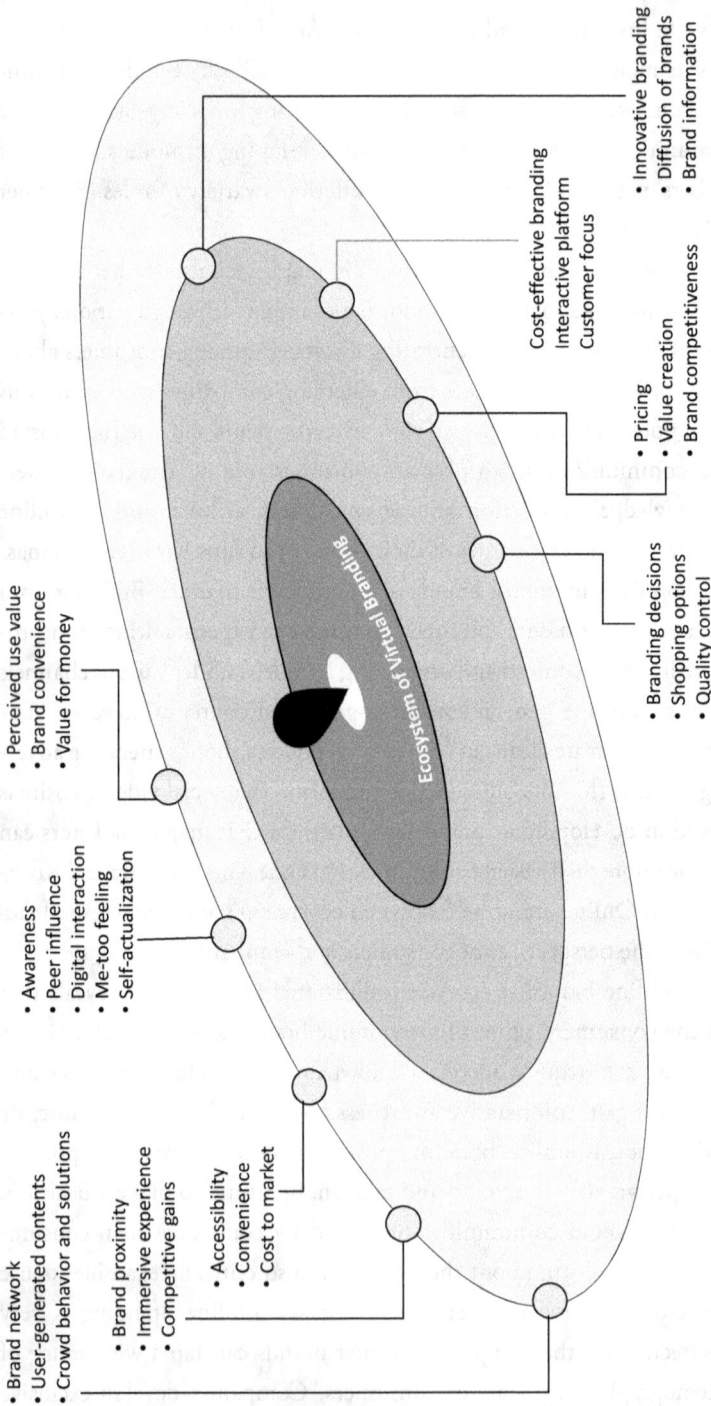

Figure 5.1 Online branding ecosystem

websites for their flagship and new emerging brands and launch brand communities targeting consumers interacting on social media.

Launching Virtual Brands

Organizations behind well-established brands in global markets have modified their brand attributes and deliverables and reconfigured them to suit region-, language-, and culture-specific consumer preferences in various destinations. Digital marketing technology has made brands more vulnerable to substitution today because of the viral effects of experience-sharing by the consumers. However, digital technology has tightened its control over brand messages through digital channels and social networks. Mergers and acquisitions have further added to the risk of brand and their associated business values overlapping creating confusion among consumers engaged in reviewing multiple brand portfolios. The relationships between brands and their customers have now become more open-ended, as online discussions extend the brand experience beyond purchase. Multinational customer-centric companies manage brand portfolios using the following strategies to stay sustainable in the marketplace:

Making brands distinctive:	Companies develop strategies to deliver relevant, distinctive, and credible value to customers. They offer benefits and experiences of brands and differentiate them through superior positioning relative to competitors. Such strategies are also used in repositioning established brands to meet customer needs effectively.
Optimizing brand portfolios and new designs:	Companies launch new brands and sub-brands continuously to compete with their rivals and serve the changing preferences of consumers, which endangers the roles and relationships of brand assets within a portfolio. Such trends in branding pose major challenges to companies in consolidating brands, reducing value-based complexity, and brand overlap.

	Brand designs should incorporate the 4As comprising attributes, availability, affordability, and adaptability.
Delivering the brand promise at all touchpoints:	Consumer-centric companies make greater efforts to deliver brand promise at all touchpoints with the customer both online and in physical deliveries. Current business dynamics and multichannel marketing environment drive companies to cocreate brand value and deliver consistent brand experience and collaborate effectively with consumers in implementing brand strategies.
Supporting consumer decisions:	Companies should be able to develop branding capabilities to guide consumers in making pro-brand decisions in response to the brand strategies of the company.

Companies in the competitive marketplace analytically measure their brand power and map current brand positions. Brand performance is commonly measured by the company in relation to the volume of sales stimulated by the effect of individual brand tactics within the brand portfolio. Companies require strong skills in optimizing marketing and brand promotion strategies to position their brand against competing brands, and the brand-line-mapping is an important part of planning exercises to be carried out to accomplish this task. Such an effort is also beneficial in identifying market segments according to customer preferences.

The brand-line should not be constant. It has to be extended over time, systematically in two ways: by stretching and by filling. The brand-line can be stretched either downward, or upward, or both ways depending upon the range of competitors and the brand-lines simultaneously existing in the market. The downward stretch results in selling the upper-end brands initially at cheaper rates on the brand-line. This strategy has to be used very carefully, as losses may pile up through a volume of out-of-fashion stock. However, the item image largely depends on the brand name. The upward stretching of the brand-line is risk-averse. Such an approach allows for selling the brand-line items at a high price, as managers are attracted by higher growth rates and profit margins. However, there always remain the threat of price "fall-out" from higher-end competitors and the threat of lower-end competitors introducing a substitute at a lower price. Finally, sales personnel of the company and its distributors must manage the crisis. The company, at the stage of "maturity" of its growth cycle, may use both upward and downward stretching of brand-line in different market segments. Adding new items or missing items on the sales stream of the market can also stretch the brand-line. The featuring of brand-line items indicates that a few of them have been selected and are being set at a high price and sales target. It may be observed that during Christmas, all consumer goods and durables are sold at relatively high prices as sales managers motivate customers to buy goods located at the higher end of the brand-line. However, in brand-line analysis, pruning is also essential to identify low-sales items on the brand-line, take them out of the marketing program, and diversify items on the brand-line to improve market competitiveness. Brand planning is done not only for consumer brands but also in many other segments of marketing, such as financial markets, social markets, and the like.

Companies frequently shift their brand's position and move to exploit less crowded territories to increase sales and overcome competition. Companies have long used perceptual mapping to understand how consumers feel about their brands relative to the competitors', to find gaps in the marketplace, and to develop brand positions. Marketing tools that measure performance of the brands include market share, growth rate, and profitability, but it is necessary for companies to map consumer perceptions about the brand so that the brand can be centrally controlled. The brand should be positioned distinctively against competing brands based on its attributes, performance, and equity in the market. Marketers should determine a brand's current and desired position, predict its marketplace performance, and devise and track marketing strategy and implementation continuously to drive brand performance. Examples of the automobile and beer markets demonstrate the use of brand-mapping tool for driving sustainable growth (Dawar and Bagga 2015).

Online Brand Positioning and Value Creation

Digital innovation, omnipresence of brands, and transparency have built customer-centricity in global brands and raised expectations across the markets at global, regional, and local levels. Many global retail brands like Calvin Klein, Tommy Hilfiger, and Zara have harnessed consumers' desire to have it all by bringing mass-market prices to the colors, fabrics, and designs of high fashion. Simultaneously, Amazon has emerged as strong customer-centric virtual brand in the digital market segment and is competing with brick-and-mortar retailers. Most digital branding companies are developing their brands close to consumer preferences by retooling their supply chains and offering innovative products and enabling faster replenishment to support the "one-day delivery" promise. Most companies are creating new advertising messages around the in-store pickup of online orders like Walmart and building their brands as customer-centric by saving the shopping time of customers. Branding companies have taken a leadership role in designing, building, and disseminating emotions into customer-experience brands like *Mercedes Me*; *Sony Like No Other*; and *Toyota's Touch the Perfection*. The digital brand platform provides customers with automated services though personalized value diagnostics for brands.

Consistency of positioning appears to be an essential criterion for success in this area. Some of the more successful brands can translate and adopt a central guiding theme such as *Just Do It* or *Always Coca-Cola*. The central theme allows the brand values to be maintained and updated or refreshed regularly. In this way, it acts as a guide for the brand. Nevertheless, there is still the possibility to express the positioning locally but within the framework of a central strategy. A brand such as Levi's or Nike can set the tone for the category. A challenger brand will need to either accept this vocabulary or compete in a new field. An example of the latter is Diesel, a brand that defines itself rather than mimicking the brand leader. However, even leader-driven brands need to be refreshed and updated. Both Nike and Adidas brands have revived not only the core sporting values but also premier sports positioning of their brands.

Brand positioning is a marketing strategy that helps a brand to stand out in the marketplace by establishing its unique value and identity in the minds of consumers. It is a way to differentiate a brand from its competitors by highlighting its unique qualities, values, and attributes. Brand positioning is a strategic process that helps a brand to create a lasting impression with its target audience, making it memorable and more desirable than other brands. Brand positioning is created by analyzing the market, competitors, and target audience to make the brand top-of-the-mind brand among consumers. This process involves developing a brand positioning statement that articulates the value propositions and differentiators against competing brands. Positioning a brand can be implemented through a variety of channels, including packaging, features, benefits, and communications. This is an ongoing process that needs to be monitored and adapted to the changing needs. It is a key part of a brand's marketing strategy that helps to shape innovation, sales, and commercialization strategies and positions the brand as the top-of-the-mind brand enabling consumers to remember it while making buying decisions.

La Colombe Coffee Roasters is an American coffee roaster and retailer with headquarters in Philadelphia. La Colombe Coffee Roasters was founded in 1994 in Philadelphia, Pennsylvania, with the tag line— *America Deserves Better Coffee*. The company provided attractive cafés and an online coffee subscription program to its customers. In 2023, it was acquired by Chobani for US$900 million as the brand has emerged as a of third-wave coffee. Third-wave coffee is often associated with the concept of specialty coffee, referring either to specialty grades of green (raw and unroasted) coffee beans (distinct from commercial-grade coffee), or specialty coffee beverages of high quality and craft. The brand recognition includes a BevNet award for Rising Star in 2017. The company supported ethical trade in the sourcing of its products and coffee innovation leading to Draft Latte cold coffee, a ready-to-drink product available in exclusive company outlets and in a variety of retail outlets. The company has developed a virtual design for its online presence and provided a seamless experience for consumers both through its cafés and online. The company has operated in a high-margin competitive industry under the risk of having to compete against low-market-share business clusters. This has led to business shutdowns in the long term. However, driving high customer interface and product innovation provided the company with fragmented opportunities to grow in selective geodemographic segments. With new equity invested by a highly successful venture capitalist, the company is now faced with the dilemma of whether to scale up into a mass-market company or to continue serving a niche segment through its artisanal cafés and innovative coffee products (Moreira et al. 2021).

Customer-centric brands influence buying decisions through emotional and rational factors. Thus, branding and sales outreach of brands account for human attributes, or customers' psychological rationale behind their buying behavior, that affect business performance. Continuous growth in the information and communication technology (ICT) has driven consumers to acquire brand knowledge at their convenience using their mobile devices. Most companies realized that brand campaigns yield effective results if channeled through mobile devices and designed around consumer personality. Customer-centric brands can be developed using communication attributes that emphasize innovativeness, personal attachment, emotions, high returns with low-risk sense among consumers, and the perceived convenience of brand acquaintance among consumers. The perceived usefulness, consumer innovativeness, and personal attachment directly influence the association of consumers with the brands. Companies seeking to build and maintain brand relationships should view these consumers personality attributes as levers to amplify consumers' acceptance toward existing and new brands (Rohm et al. 2012). Accordingly, most consumer electronics companies make sure that customers not only see their televisions and listen to audio systems in stores but also learn about their vivid high-definition pictures by sharing consumer experiences. Following the market-trend, Amazon. com began offering targeted product recommendations to consumers already logged into the virtual store and ready to buy. Much before the customer-centric brand-building trend became a success tool in the market, Procter & Gamble had initiated radio and then television programs to enable its brands reach target audiences through sponsorship of various *soap operas* that were emotionally appealing for consumers.

Titan Industries Ltd. in India made the first attempt in early 1990s to introduce a watch brand exclusively for women with the brand name "Titan Raga." This brand was launched with an appeal to trendy women to grow with time and stay symbolic to the Indian culture. The company targeted customers who were progressive homemakers in the transforming society and trying to balance work and family life. This customer segment was found to be most suited for this brand, as consumers in this segment was looking to embellish their traditional or Western attire with a beautiful, sensual timepiece. After the millennium break, the

customer profile for "Titan Raga" brand switched to young career professionals with higher disposable income, and the brand significance shifted
from "heritage and beauty" to "self-esteem and romance." Accordingly,
this brand has reached a new stage of its customer-centric journey, going
beyond its consumers' earlier perception about the watches as an orna-
mental and a sort of exotic gift with accentuated feminine qualities to
women. As more global brands penetrated in India by 2010, the company wanted to strengthen its customer-centric branding strategy to meet
the new branding challenges to compete. The brand ambassadors of the
company carried out campaigns to promote sustainable brand image in
keeping with changing consumer profile, and the company could successfully drive the standalone brand strategy for "Titan Raga" to distinguish it
from the growing competition in the industry.

The emergence of social networking applications such as Myspace,
Twitter (now X), and Facebook have reduced the distance between business firms and their consumers in B-to-C as well as in B-to-B segments.
Most traditional communications media including telephone, music,
film, and television are reshaped or redefined by the Internet and new
services such as Voice over Internet Protocol (VoIP) and Internet Protocol
Television (IPTV). Newspaper, book, and other forms of print publishing are adapting to website technology or are reshaped into blogging and
web feeds. The Internet has enabled and accelerated new forms of human
interactions through instant messaging, Internet forums, and social networking. Online shopping has boomed both for major retail outlets and
small artisans and traders. B-to-B and financial services on the Internet
affect supply chains across entire industries (Rajagopal 2013).

Brand Empowerment

Brand empowerment concept is evolving into true participatory conversations with growth in technology and user-friendly communication devises available to consumers. Besides technology adaptation in branding
communications, controlled brand communications with distinct and
corporate spokespeople may give a free way to business communications
consisting of multiple players, including customers, competitors, observers, and employees. Amidst this, the consumer-generated content (CGC)

is based on cocreation of information, which is more beneficial to the firms than company-driven market communications. The true reward in CGC is that the process and the outcome are not reliant on technical prowess but are semiotic and narrative in disseminating the information. Consumers, especially those who are members of active consumer collectives, are skillful, proficient, and prolific in the creation of CGC, with high resonance among very engaged consumers (Muniz and Schau 2011). The liberal communication rules are augmented by simple communication technologies, and a lack of legal barriers to sharing information creates rich common knowledge, the ability to organize teams modularly, extraordinary motivation, and high levels of trust, all of which radically lower transaction costs.

Brands can be empowered to perform satisfactorily in the market by combining strategic communications and strategic brand management. This approach to empower brands helps companies develop integrated branding communications (IBC) and deliver holistic consumer experience. Accordingly, the key mission of IBC is to manage effectively the mediated impression of, and direct encounter with, the brand so that synergism ensues among all the interrelated elements of IBC, including research and development, manufacturing, price formulation, channel arrangement, consumer service management, branding message construction, and communication program execution. As such, IBC can enhance the holistic consumer experience creating a holistic brand value structure that can unite the consumer's sensory, emotional, social, and intellectual experiences in a new and positive way. A conceptual framework on communication attributes argues that communication process is based on the foundation of two fundamental premises—AIDA and ACCA. The variable of Attention, Interest, Desire, and Action constitutes the AIDA concept, while Awareness, Comprehension, Conviction, and Action are integrated in the ACCA paradigm of consumer behavior. The main AIDA influence is the ability of advertisement to hold attention and drive the subject into action. AIDA factors also help retailing firms and brands sustain market competition and make advertisements more memorable, enhancing brand awareness particularly for desired products (Premeaux 2006).

Marketers can gain consumers' attention by product samples, large visual signs, and other sensory techniques. Once the marketer has the consumer's attention, they must craft their interest through product information and consumer communications. ACCA paradigm of consumer behavior argues that awareness on sales promotions in convergence with advertisement content generates conviction among consumers who lean toward action resulting in store choice and buying decisions (Rajagopal 2011). It is believed that consumers' strong conviction about buying decisions can be effectively brought into an action, provided it is based on accurate and acceptable information. Given the great potential of brand campaigns delivered via mobile devices and the evolution of near-field communication technologies, it has been observed that the factors influencing consumers' acceptance of untethered, or mobile, branding across three influential markets: the United States, China, and Europe. It is necessary for firms to examine the extent to which the usefulness of mobile information/programs and individual characteristics such as innovativeness, personal attachment, and risk avoidance influence attitudes of consumers toward mobile branding. It has been observed that perceived usefulness, consumer innovativeness, and personal attachment with brands directly influence attitudes toward mobile branding in all three markets. In China and Europe, risk avoidance also negatively influences attitudes toward mobile branding. Marketers seeking to build and maintain customer relationships via mobile platforms should focus on these individual characteristics to amplify consumers' acceptance of mobile branding (Rohm et al. 2012). Social media is good for branding from many points of view. Smart companies are exploring how to use this information channel internally to infuse peer-to-peer collaboration. Most firms involving social media as a branding-communication channel tap the knowledge and expertise of consumers for mutual benefit and brand-building process more than a traditional knowledge management approach, where people dump their information in a giant database that nobody reads. Such firms can create an environment where they go through peer-to-peer collaboration. Emerging firms may initially build very small collaborative tools that could enable their peer communication design to kick off the consumer–company collaboration process and to get experience in understanding how it provides mutual benefits. They had successes built upon other successes in terms of effectiveness of networks with customers.

Hybrid Brand Promotion

Lifebuoy, one of the flagship family brands of carbolic soap from Hindustan Unilever Limited (HUL), has completed the brand journey of over 130 years. The strong-smelling, dull, red soap, which was first introduced in 1895 in India, has come to life through the energetic advertisements and embedded jingle on radio, television, and cinema halls with the tune of *Tandurusti ki raksha karta hai Lifebuoy* (Lifebuoy protects the health). Since its inception, the brand has been regarded as the ultimate bathing soap for men who are engaged in physical labor. As other competing brands appeared in the market over time, HLL considered repositioning the brand to deliver a new brand experience to consumers and strengthen its brand equity in 2002. The challenge for Lifebuoy was to bring the desired change, while retaining its core disinfectant properties. So, the core positioning strategy was moved from men battling grime and dirt to mothers chasing a healthy soap to protect children from mild dermatological infections caused by reckless playing. In 2004, Lifebuoy was re-launched with four variants under one "umbrella"—brand value. The variants included Lifebuoy Strong, Lifebuoy Fresh, Lifebuoy Gold, and Lifebuoy Naturals that delivered a distinct experience over the conventional form of the brand and reinforced confidence among consumers. Since 2011, the brand has further evolved, and Lifebuoy started being sold on a "seasonal" platform with the brand campaign on "Protection from 10 infection causing germs." The 10 infections identified include flu, sore throat, respiratory infection, dysentery, diarrhea, rash, skin infection, sore eyes, acne, and ear infection. This new brand platform has given a new healthy experience of the soap as a family health product.[4]

Singapore Airlines uses brand metrics and score card tools to periodically evaluate its brand and stay ahead of competition. The airline company has decided on a fully branded product/service value to differentiate its brand drivers, which include innovation, value of technology, and quality of customer service, from its competitors. Innovation is considered as an important constituent of the brand, and ergonomics combined

---

[4]Corporate website of Hindustan Unilever Limited. https://www.hul.co.in/brands/personal-care/lifebuoy/.

with in-flight customer experience are key factors of their success. The company has priority to take delivery of new aircraft types and introduce sub-brands like 747-Megatop and 777-Jubilee to further distinguish its brand from competitors. Brand strategy of Singapore Airlines is, in principle, a relatively high-cost strategy. Each brand requires significant investment, careful management, and detailed implementation programs to live up to the brand promise. The airlines company has carefully built a financial and fixed cost infrastructure, which allows them to continue investing to support the brand and command a price premium through consistent brand benefits.

Branding Strategies

A firm's effectiveness may be identified based on its operational and system competencies. Operational competency refers to the technical competency demonstrated in production, packaging, distribution, quality control, and information management. Cost-efficiency largely depends on technical competency. System competency includes value assurance, value enhancement, and innovation. A company may move its position of the product to the quadrant where the effectiveness of the company and the unit cost remain high due to improved technological and branding interventions. However, in a situation where the unit cost of the product and effectiveness of the organizations are low, the growth rate would slow down, and strategies need to be built to revive the growth first and then embark on efforts to sustain the firm's position against competition. In case of high unit cost of the product and low effectiveness of the organization, none of the competitive strategies would prove worth due to nonviability of economy of scale. The company must make decisions mainly on either diversifying its activities or paying more attention to strengthening its brand base. In this decision-making process, the company must consider some important variables like spillover effects in terms of supply backlog, product improvement, packaging, price sensitivity, and operational problems, including cost of distribution and margin spread. The company should measure the brand performance of product, effective consumer response in terms of sales, and customers' convenience in terms of access to the product. The process of building competitive brand strategy takes substantial time and needs to be assessed and reassessed through careful analyses. It is essential that the action required to implement the selected strategy needs to be prioritized and documented. Strategy is a not a task of one point of time; it is, and should be, a continuous process. The company should follow the checklist of activities in building the strategy for competitive branding as stated below:

- Scanning of environment;
- Identifying relevant economic inevitable and rigid factors;
- Identifying the key trends of major competing brands;
- Identifying political, economic, sociocultural, and technological factors affecting the product market;
- Conducting an activity cost analysis for the upstream and down-stream linkages with the company;
- Identifying the core competency of the company;
- Reviewing the statistical resources of the company's operational and human resources;
- Preparing mission and key strategies;
- Identifying culture and leadership style;
- Identifying competitive position;
- Making adjustment and acquaintance with government policies;
- Determining levels of cost in production and operations;
- Designing price levels and consumer segments;
- Identifying strength of demand for the product;
- Identifying opportunities for expansion of the product line and the brand; and
- Preparing contingency plans of branding.

Building appropriate brand-mix for strategy development is a difficult task for multi-brand companies. It becomes more challenging for companies while introducing their brands into chaotic markets like India, where market competition is very high. Chinese corporation Haier Inc., the biggest seller of major appliances in the world, has entered India in 2006. Its global presence restores the credibility of its brand to position the brand as a high-value innovation-driven brand, but Indian consumers have yet to develop the willingness to embrace its China-made, high-priced products. Haier brands are facing such dichotomy in its business endeavors in India for a decade, which has caused Haier brands to suffer sluggish sale and narrow market share. The company then undertook to revive its brand-mix in reference to price, place, and promotion and refurbished its marketing infrastructure to save its market. Companies need to configure marketing and localization strategies carefully in emerging markets like India. The brand-mix also incorporates brand offerings, brand communication, pricing strategies, and brand engagement strategies by providing brand services (Celly and Lau 2012). In a brand, service firms focus on building customer-brand relationships, emphasizing the embedded brand promise and consistent experiences. Key strategies of brand service include value enhancement, consumer awareness, standardizing its delivery, and leveraging unique benefits like customer-centricity.

Dimensions of Brand-Scope Strategies

Brand-scope strategy deals with market coverage. A business unit may serve an entire brand or concentrate on one or more of its parts. Three major alternatives in brand-scope strategy are single-brand strategy, multi-brand strategy, and total-brand strategy. A variety of reasons may lead a company to focus its efforts on a single segment of the market. For example, a small company may find a unique niche in a market and spend resources in serving this niche. The *single-brand strategy* consists of seeking out a market segment that is considered too small, too risky, or just plain unappealing by larger competitors. The strategy does not work in areas where the brand power of big companies is important in realizing economies of scale, as in the extractive and process industries. Companies concentrating on a single brand have the advantage of being able to make quick responses to brand opportunities and threats through appropriate changes in policies. The single-brand (or niche) strategy is an outcome of necessity. As far as the impact of the single-brand strategy is concerned, it affects profitability in a positive direction. When effort is concentrated on a single brand, particularly when competition is minimal, it is feasible to keep costs down and product price high, thus earning substantially higher profits. The large companies in many distinct segments implement the *multi-brand strategy*. It is necessary to choose such brand segments that have low competition and pro-brand consumer attitude to enable the company to implement the multi-brand strategy successfully. This strategy may be implemented either by selling different products in different brand segments or by arranging distribution of the same product in many segments.

A company uses the *house-of-brands strategy* to serve an entire brand by selling different products directed toward different segments of the market. Companies employ house-of-brand strategy either to create corporate brand or reinforce the existing corporate brand. A key success factor in developing the house-of-brand strategy is to create emotional links between the corporate brand, individual brands, and consumer reaction. The corporate brand is built through design innovation, working with a safe and diverse employee environment, customer-centered manufacturing, and delivering corporate social responsibility. The Whirlpool corporate brand has a history dating back to 1911. The company has steadily expanded its product line, revenues, and global footprint for more than six decades as evident by returns on milestone. Whirlpool Corporation offers a wide range of household appliance products, including washing machines, clothes dryers, refrigerators, freezers, cooking appliances, microwave ovens, dishwashers, and a complete range of built-in appliances. Within these product lines, the company has also established a portfolio of brands through innovative product design, targeted marketing, and a spectrum of partnerships with trade customers. This portfolio enables the company to offer multiple brands with distinct values in the same product category. A prime example is the company's "house of brands" for kitchen appliances, which includes the following brands:

- KitchenAid—an upmarket brand serving professional chefs and the "home enthusiast or entertainer";
- Whirlpool—a mass-market brand serving families and, in particular, the "active balancer" or "super-mom." Branding for Whirlpool appliances includes taglines such as "cook more," "style and performance unite," and "Form. Function. Unity";

- Roper—a value brand serving cost-conscious consumers who buy based on price. Branding for Roper appliances includes taglines such as "sensible solutions for your family" and "simple, sturdy, affordable workhorse appliances."

A company may start with a single product. As the brand grows and as different segments emerge, leading competitors may attempt to compete in all segments by offering different combinations of product, price, promotion, and distribution strategies. Companies following the house-of-brand strategy attempt to enter new segments as they discover market demand. The leading companies may themselves create new segments and try to control them from the outset. The total-brand strategy is highly risky. So, a very small number of companies in an industry may intend to follow it. A company needs substantial financial, physical, and human resources to implement this strategy in many brand segments at the same time. Thus, only the companies in a strong financial position may find this strategy attractive. Chrysler Corporation's financial woes in the 1990s led it to reduce the scope of its brands overseas at a time when experts were anticipating the emergence of a single global brand. The total-brand strategy can be highly rewarding in terms of achieving growth and brand share, but it may or may not lead to increased profitability.

The company needs to assess the strengths and weaknesses of its existing brands before making the branding decision for their product. A manufacturing company may have several options on brand sponsorship. The product may be launched as a retail private brand or as manufacturer's brand. A distributor brand can also be considered for retailing—for example, edible oils, sugar, processed grains, and in many other products that need repacking or licensed brand names. For many years, multinational corporations have been competing successfully in the market within their multi-brand segments by exploiting market share of product and scope of branding. These companies took advantage of customer preferences to create brand value and reputation in the market. But these ways of competing with brands are no longer profitable to companies, as there is a continuous growth of new competing brands posing threats to existing brands. Under such multi-brand competition, it is hard for companies to sustain an advantage based on conventional branding strategies. Companies must seek new sources of brand advantage and position their brands aggressively in the competitive marketplace. Building brands in a near-monopolistic situation has been easier for companies to capitalize on the attributes of brands in the market. However, in the marketing era of 21st century, companies are engaged in developing regional brands by exploring the scope of branding through collaboration with local companies and consumers. Developing collaboration with potential companies on branding has emerged as a major tool to enhance the scope of competitive brands in the late 20th century (Rajagopal 2019).

Co-branding is being increasingly used by companies of both large and small sizes to raise consumer awareness and generate sales. At the most basic level, businesses use a consumer-centric approach based on the user complementarity and preferences, which reflects their interest and efforts toward enhancing their current brand-lines. For example, Hershey's Syrup added to Betty Crocker Brownies is an example of combined technologies that seek to create an entirely new product; another example is the Sports Kit by Nike and Apple. Many companies embark on co-branding programs as this has been experienced during the 1990s as a powerful way of introducing a company's products and services to loyal consumers of another company. Perhaps the best example of this is the legendary "Intel Inside" campaign, which was launched after the success of the co-branding, Intel had expanded its scope of co-branding with as many as 300 computer manufacturers. Another benefit of co-branding has become evident for companies toward cost-savings on sales and services infrastructure. Hence, increasingly growing fast-food restaurants like Pizza Hut and Taco Bell that belong to Yum Brands Inc. tend to share the same building and often the same counter, menu boards, and staff to serve their customers (McKee 2009). Several barriers impede collaboration within complex multiunit organizations. To overcome those barriers, companies develop distinct organizing capabilities that cannot be easily imitated. Companies can develop framework that links managerial action, barriers to inter-unit collaboration, and value creation in multinational corporations to help managers understand how collaborative advantage can work. This framework can conceptualize collaboration and co-branding as a set of management levers to several types of value creation.

Brand Cocreation

The plethora of strategies used by companies to cocreate brands today is spread across Facebook, YouTube, blogs, and other social network platforms. Such strategies endorse the new paradigm known as cocreation. Cocreation is the process by which products, services, and experiences are developed jointly by companies and their stakeholders to enhance their product value, brand equity, and belongingness of their brand among consumers. Though the cocreation process is increasingly being employed by certain progressive organizations, individuals appear to be more empowered to embrace the cocreation of brands. Companies must seek to engage people as active cocreators of brands and enhance their value on every front. Cocreating experience can be initiated by companies through dialogues on brands, accessibility, evaluation of the risk-benefit status of the brand, and conveying the transparency of brands in reference to the promises made by the brands. In 2008, *Tchibo*, a German coffee and consumer goods corporation, launched *Tchibo* Ideas, an Internet platform where customers can share their product and brand design ideas with the company. The business of LEGO, a global brand for creative children's toys, has moved from a traditional product-centric *make and sell* business model to a more customer-centric "anticipate and lead" model in which products are cocreated with customers, and customers are leveraged as a key factor in the company's innovation strategy.

With growing social media consciousness among consumers and stakeholders, most consumer-centric companies, irrespective of whether they have crowdfunding, tend to invest increasingly on brand communication using social media channels. Consequently, firms allocate enormous budgets to establish their new and flagship brands and maintain a social media presence. Firms have discovered many interactive ways on social media that not only motivate crowd movements on customer preferences but also invite, promote, and display user-generated content on their online and social media platforms. New experiments on crowd-based brand communications on prominent channels like Facebook and Instagram rapidly affect customers' behavior. The "likes" on a brand drive customers to discretely follow it and allure people more likely to purchase it. The number of "likes" not only affects family and friends but also drives the community at large to lean toward making buying decisions. Interactions on social media inculcate crowd cognition, collective intelligence, and conscious consumption behavior in the long run among users of social media channels, while the "like" and "follow" options affect their short-run purchasing. For example, social media may persuade people to engage in social health and well-being behaviors in the long run. However, the "likes" need to be checked for manipulations and unethical disruptions to influence people adversely (John et al. 2017). Over time, these social media channels turned out to be the hubs for crowdsourcing, opinion building, and cocreating innovations. Firms with goals to attract a large number of customers to their brands made high investment on advertisements developed with their own creative content, but the response of customers has been less than the level anticipated. In fact, social media seems to have made such brands less significant. Social media channels stimulated crowd cultures and promoted the alternative approach of cultural branding (Holt 2016).

Word-of-mouth is another potential way to acquire new customers as well as to retain existing customers through building loyalty and trust on brand and company. On the contrary, this media may also lay negative effects among peers by spewing dissatisfaction within the segment. Such developments in word-of-mouth platforms may even push firms to lose consumers (Yu 2007). In addition, companies benefit from cocreation process in socializing their existing and upcoming brands by developing referrals and brand gatekeepers in the societal niche, which helps in enhancing the customer outreach. Societal engagement of business corporations opens avenues to enter downstream markets alongside mass and premium market segments, driving them to conquer the universe of market (comprising premium, upper mass, regular mass, lower mass, and bottom-of-the-pyramid market segment). In an interactive social and business environment, coevolution of businesses with societal values provides competitive leverage to companies and helps in achieving corporate social identity.

Rapidly emerging new brands (with crowd-based ideas) from unfamiliar companies attract consumers by offering low prices. Although most consumers tend to experiment with low-priced products and substitute products that deliver satisfactory experience, they fail to develop sustainable perceptions and build attitude toward repeat buying. However, industry attractiveness reflects competition among traditional pipeline brands that succeed by optimizing activities in their value chains. In addition, crowdsourcing and collective intelligence have helped companies and their brand to streamline customer perceptions, brand value, and competitiveness. Uber (transport service), Alibaba (e-commerce), and Airbnb (urban housing) are growing in the market by improving the consumer chain and delivering satisfaction through active customer engagement and collective intelligence (Van Alstyne et al. 2016). Positive psychodynamics among consumers creates pull-effect for specific brands in the market. The pull-effect generates high consumer demand, which benefits companies in increasing market share and profit by reducing marketing costs. Such costs for brands are spread across advertisements, in-store promotions, price discounts, and point-of-sales incentives to consumers. The psychodynamics also generates referrals and brand advocacy behavior among consumers, which helps companies acquire new consumers at a relatively low cost.

Case Study

CS1: Interactive Brand Promotion: Heineken USA

Heineken, a Dutch brewing company, used an interactive video as an interactive marketing tool for a part of a HR campaign in 2016 to showcase the work culture in the company and visualizing it an employee-friendly environment. The video illustrated the fun company culture with focus on freedom to work in a de-stressing corporate work culture.[5] The video shows recruiters checking the personality of candidates and introducing them to the corporate work culture of the firm. In the video, the employer asks 12 questions the answers to which let candidates decide whether they are a good fit for Heineken. The interactive marketing campaign has gone viral, and the company has seen an increase in the number of applicants by three times. The engagement statistics have shown that this interactive campaign had crowd appeal and 67 percent of the users took all the tests

---

[5]For details see Heineken video on You Tube. https://www.youtube.com/watch?v=0QoGzV72wR8.

and spent nearly 7 minutes watching the video. This marketing campaign not only focused on the recruitment needs and corporate ambience but also promoted proximity of crowd to the company.

In addition, Heineken launched a global campaign featuring a bottle opener that instantly shuts down all work appliances as the bottle of Heineken is opened. The video titled "The Closer" addresses a growing work–life imbalance in the busy corporate work culture and inspires them to stop overworking.[6] Dramatizing the campaign through the video appeal, the film delivers the solutions to the always-on work culture. Heineken brand emphasizes that this proximity video is based on crowd sentiments and hidden problems, needs, and solution-related factors. "The Closer" bottle opener empowers employees through this media to have a work–life balance. This campaign explores the PNS (problems, needs, and solutions) factors to reach out to customers and reaffirm the proximity of the company to the people. The video begins with an office employee stuck in a meeting, unable to meet his friend who is at a party. Leveraging this opportunity to introduce both its Heineken bottles and the bottle opener, the employee then finds that with the opening of the bottle all work appliances begin shutting down and the office becomes totally dark. As the video progresses, it showcases the same happening at different places where employees are working, including in a world summit, news broadcast room, and even a bar. Consequently, the video ends with employees being able to take a break from their work and enjoy themselves while holding Heineken bottles.

Heineken promotes proximity marketing and manages changing relationships with customers and stakeholders through carefully crafted social media campaigns such as #ShareTheSofa and #ChampionTheMatch. These initiatives support marketing efforts by enhancing proximity to people and delivering online interactions through boosting brand awareness and positioning the brand among target customers. The company's popular social media platform is Facebook, where it has generated over 20 million Likes, and the company has optimized the Facebook page with a geotargeting approach. Heineken serves content-specific communication

---

[6]For details see Heineken video on You Tube. https://www.youtube.com/watch?v= cP3JRx4p9BQ&t=7s.

to their Facebook fans, which are aggregated by the general Likes trend to exhibit impressive results. In 2012, Brazil Fan page launched a famous real-time campaign called *One Like One Balloon*, which turned out to be incredibly successful in producing spectacular fan engagement and following. The idea behind such proximity marketing campaign was to answer to every new Page Like by blowing up a green balloon and placing it in the Brazilian Heineken's office space. The office space got full in just 1 (symbolically) day, and this initiative had driven enormous user-generated content in addition to more than 1 million new Fans in a short time.

Summary

Discussions in this chapter are woven around the theme of virtual branding and form the core of thematic deliberations. Some important aspects of developing online brands and different strategies to launch virtual brands have been discussed in detail. In addition, the brand strategies associated with competitive brand positioning and value creation have been discussed thoroughly. It is argued that brands are successful also because people prefer them over unbranded products. In addition to the psychological factors already mentioned, brands give consumers the means whereby they can make choices and judgments. Bases on these experiences, customers can then rely on chosen brands to guarantee standards of quality and service, which reduces the risk of failure in purchase. Today's world is characterized by complex technology, and this can be extremely confusing to people who are not technology-minded. Brands can play an important role by providing simplicity and reassurance and offering a quick, clear guide to a variety of competitive products. It may be stated that animism is another process mechanism that directly explains the specific ways in which the vitality of the brand can be realized. Over time, personalities of the spokespersons are transmitted to the brand. Obviously, this aspect is much less under the control of marketers and indirectly the brand personality is created by all the elements of the marketing-mix. The personality of a brand is created over time, by all the constituents of marketing-mix.

This chapter also discusses the concept of virtual brand advocacy through experiential marketing, collective consumerism, advocacy patterns, and future shopping trends. Building acquaintance with the virtual brands, developing brand communities, and architecting crowd-based branding have been discussed. Cocreation as a customer-centric branding strategy for e-commerce brands has been discussed at length. A case study on interactive brand promotion initiated by Heineken Beer in the United States bridges the theories, concepts, and applications of brand building, launching, and positioning discussed in this chapter.

References

Avery, J., and R. Nahas. 2021. *Camera IQ and the Metaverse: Building Augmented Reality Brand Experiences.* Harvard Business School Publication.

Barwise, P., and S. Meehan. 2010. "The One Thing You Must Get Right When Building a Brand." *Harvard Business Review* 88 (12): 80–4.

Bu, L. 2015. "Can Brands Control Their Online Destiny." *McKinsey Insights,* December.

Celly, N., and P. Lau. 2012. *Haier in India: Building Presence in a Mass Market Beyond China.* Cambridge, MA: Harvard Business School Press.

Dawar, N., and C. Bagga. 2015. "A Better Way to Map Brand Strategy." *Harvard Business Review* 93 (6): 90–7.

Fournier, S., and L. Lee. 2009. "Getting Brand Communities Right." *Harvard Business Review* 87 (4): 105–11.

Holt, D. B. 2016. "Branding in the Age of Social Media." *Harvard Business Review* 94 (3): 40–50.

John, L. K., O., Emrich, S., Gupta, and M. I. Norton. 2017. "Does 'Liking' Lead to Loving? The Impact of Joining a Brand's Social Network on Marketing Outcomes." *Journal of Marketing Research* 54 (1): 144–55.

McKee, S. 2009. "The Pros-And Cons of Co-Branding." *Bloomberg Business Online,* July 10.

Moreira, S., R. Mudambi, and V. Sreenivas. 2021. *La Colombe Coffee: The Tangible and Intangible Elements of Brand Identity.* Cambridge, MA: Harvard Business School Publication.

Muniz, A. M., and H. J. Schau. 2011. "How to Inspire Value-Laden Collaborative Consumer-Generated Content." *Business Horizons* 54 (3): 209–17.

Premeaux, S. R. 2006. "The Attitudes of Middle-Class Male and Female Consumers Regarding the Effectiveness of Celebrity Endorsers." *Journal of Promotion Management* 11 (4): 33–48.

Rajagopal. 2011. "Impact of Radio Advertisements on Buying Behavior of Urban Commuters." *International Journal of Retail and Distribution Management* 39 (7): 480–503.

Rajagopal. 2013. *Managing Social Media and Consumerism: The Grapevine Effect in Competitive Markets*. Basingstoke, UK: Palgrave Macmillan.

Rajagopal. 2019. *Competitive Branding Strategies: Managing Performance in Emerging Markets*. Cham, Switzerland: Springer.

Rohm, A. J., T. Gao, F. Sultan, and M. Pagani. 2012. "Brand in the Hand: A Cross-Market Investigation of Consumer Acceptance of Mobile Branding." *Business Horizons* 55 (5): 485–93.

Roy, S., and Y. L. R. Moorthi. 2012. *Amar Chitra Katha: Changing the Brand with Changing Times*. Cambridge, MA: Harvard Business School Press.

Teixeira, T. S., and L. Kornfeld. 2014. *YouTube for Brands*. Cambridge, MA: Harvard Business School Press.

Van Alstyne, M. W., G. Parker, and S. P. Choudary. 2016. "Pipelines, Platforms, and the New Rules of Strategy." *Harvard Business Review* 94 (4): 54–62.

Yu, L. 2007. "The Quality Effect on Word-of-Mouth." *Sloan Management Review* 49 (1): 7.

About the Author

Dr. Rajagopal is distinguished professor of marketing at EGADE Business School of Tecnologico de Monterrey (ITESM), at Mexico City Campus, and Fellow of the Royal Society for Encouragement of Arts, Manufacture and Commerce, London. He is also Fellow of the Chartered Management Institute, and Fellow of Institute of Operations Management, United Kingdom. He has been a visiting professor at Boston University, Boston, Massachusetts, since 2013. He has been listed with biography in various international directories.

Dr. Rajagopal holds postgraduate and doctoral degrees in economics and marketing, respectively, from Pandit Ravishankar Shukla University in India. His specialization is in the field of marketing management. He has to his credit 82 books on marketing management and rural development themes and over 450 research contributions that include published research papers in national and international refereed journals. He is editor-in-chief of *International Journal of Leisure and Tourism Marketing* and *International Journal of Business Competition and Growth*. Dr. Rajagopal was the associate editor of *Emerald Emerging Markets Case Studies* (2012–2019), published by Emerald Publishers, United Kingdom. He is on the editorial board of various journals of international repute.

Dr. Rajagopal has been conferred the honor of Distinguished Professor by the EGADE Business School, Mexico, in 2020. His research contributions have been recognized by the National Council of Science and Technology (CONACyT), Government of Mexico, by awarding him the highest level of National Researcher-SNI Level-III in 2013. He has been awarded UK-Mexico Visiting Chair 2016–2017 for collaborative research on "Global-Local Innovation Convergence" with University of Sheffield, UK, instituted by the Consortium of Higher Education Institutes of Mexico and UK.

Dr. Rajagopal has been conferred the Overseas Indian Award (*Pravasi Bhartiya Samman Award*) in January 2023 for his outstanding contribution in the field of education. This is the highest honor conferred by the President of India. This award has been conferred in acknowledgment of the outstanding achievement in the field of education in India, United States, and Mexico.

Index

www.ingramcontent.com/pod-product-compliance
Lightning Source LLC
Chambersburg PA
CBHW061212220326
41599CB00025B/4616